RULERS
OF NEW
TESTAMENT TIMES

RULERS
OF NEW
TESTAMENT TIMES

Charles Ludwig

A Division of B/P Publications
Denver Colorado 80215

MEMBER OF
EVANGELICAL CHRISTIAN
PUBLISHERS ASSOCIATION

ACCENT BOOKS
A Division of B/P Publications
12100 W. Sixth Avenue
Denver, Colorado 80215

Copyright © 1976 B/P Publications, Inc.
Printed in U.S.A.

Library of Congress Catalog Card Number: 75-40910

ISBN 0-916406-15-6

Preface

Any book that helps bring the New Testament to life is a valuable book. And to do that is the main purpose of *Rulers of New Testament Times*. This book attempts to do that in several ways.

One of the great scenes of the New Testament is when Jesus stood as a prisoner before Herod Antipas. This was God in the hands of a man! Ah, but the drama increases for the modern man when he learns that this Herod was the son of the Herod who tried to kill the infant Jesus. And the drama gets a further nudge when we realize that that Herod had also had trouble with the Sanhedrin. Indeed, he had had so much trouble with that august body, he had ordered forty-five of them put to death!

Or, let us take a look at Paul as he stood bound before Felix. Here, again, the drama tightens when we learn that Felix was a former slave; and that even during the trial he was in such deep trouble with the Roman government he feared for his life.

This book is not intended for the scholar. Such a person needs something far more technical than this. Rather, it is intended for the serious reader interested in New Testament background. And if from this book you can find an hour or two of pleasure or a few windows with which to illuminate a sermon or Sunday School lesson, I shall feel amply rewarded.

Charles Ludwig
Tucson, Arizona

For Doctor Max Gaulke

Credits

The author wishes to express his thanks to the following publishers for granting permission to quote from their works.

E. P. Dutton, New York, for "Pliny's Letter to Trajan," from *Private Letters, Pagan and Christian,* by Dorothy Brooke. Copyright 1930 by E. P. Dutton, Inc.; renewal 1958 by Lady Dorothy Brooke.

Penguin Books Ltd., London, for quotations from *The History of the Church from Christ to Constantine* (pages 111, 126, 161, 162), translated by G. A. Williamson (Penguin Classics 1965). Copyright 1965 by G. A. Williamson.

Simon and Schuster, New York, for quotations from *Caesar and Christ* by Will Durant. Copyright 1944 by Will Durant.

A. P. Watt & Son, London, for quotations from *The Twelve Caesars* by Suetonius, translated by Robert Graves and published by Penguin Classics. Permission granted by Robert Graves. Copyright 1957.

Illustrations

Contents

CHAPTER 1

Herod the Great

He murdered his wife, executed his sons, attempted to kill Jesus, and twice tried to commit suicide. Nevertheless, history calls him Herod the Great. And in a sense, history is right!

Grossly immoral, he had ten wives—two of them nieces—and had affairs with his own eunuchs. Likewise, he was the source of the numerous Herods who cast such sinister shadows throughout the New Testament. Sorting and identifying these Herods is an intriguing task. But it is worthwhile—even though it is something like learning the names of different types of spiders.

Undoubtedly the best way to understand the Herods is to start with Herod the Great. But first we must think of his grandfather Antipas and his father Antipater.

Antipas was the first of the Herods to come to public notice. We do not know much about him. He was, however, designated "general over all Idumea." The beginnings of his son Antipater are also shrouded in mystery. But we do know that he held high political position and that he lived in Jerusalem around 67 B.C. Amazingly, Antipater was not a racial Jew, nor was his wife Cypros! Antipater, father of Herod the Great, the King of the Jews, was an Edomite. These descendants of

Herod the Great

Esau occupied the deserts of Southern Judea. And from the beginning of their existence they had been antagonistic to Israel. They had a habit of swooping down on Jewish settlements and making slaves of the people.

Indeed, the Edomites were such a problem they were denounced by the prophets: Amos, Joel, Obadiah, and Ezekiel. A psalmist also pointedly wrote: "Remember, O Lord, the children of Edom in the day of Jerusalem; who said, Rase it, rase it, even to the foundation thereof" (Psalm 137:7).

The Edomites, however, had been conquered in the second century B.C. by the Jewish high priest and king, John Hyrcanus. Hyrcanus then forced them to be circumcised and to become Jews. Thus, Antipater was a Jew merely because his ancestors had been forced into Judaism.

And yet even more damaging to the children of Antipater in the sight of the Jews was the fact that his wife was a Nabatean Arab! And even worse, according to Jewish law, the children took the nationality of the mother. Still, this is not the end of the handicaps that were heaped on the shoulders of the future King of the Jews. Antipater had five children. Four of these: Phasael, Joseph, Salome, and Pheroras had solid Jewish names. But alas, when the King-to-be of the Jews made his appearance in 73 B.C. he was shackled with the Greek name Herod!

With a Greek name, an Arab mother, and an Edomite father, young Herod should have stayed out of politics—especially Jewish politics. But Herod possessed an agile mind and such hindrances meant nothing to him.

After clearing the Mediterranean of pirates in 63 B.C., Pompey headed for Jerusalem. Fearing for the life of his ten-year-old son Herod, Antipater sent him along with his mother to Petra. There, he was undoubtedly taunted by the Arabian children as being a Jew, just as he was taunted by the children in Jerusalem as being an Arab. These taunts were like a knife and they twisted deep into his heart. And then he had an experience that influenced his entire future life.

Petra was close to the Dead Sea and not too far from the place where, two thousand years later, the Dead Sea Scrolls were found; and thus Essenes were a familiar sight on the streets. While on his way to school, Herod was surprised when a distinguished Essene by the name of Menahem approached. While patting him on his behind, the old man said that he was glad to meet the future King of the Jews.

"But I am just a commoner," replied Herod. He was a little startled for Menahem had a reputation of knowing the future.

"You will nevertheless become the king," assured the old man, "and you will reign happily because God has found you worthy." Then, arching his great brows, he added a word of caution. "Your most reasonable course of action, which will bring you a good reputation, will be to practice justice and piety toward God. *But I know you will not be such a person.*"

Young Herod grew rapidly into a tall, good looking young man. He had powerful shoulders, was good with a bow and arrow; and he was an expert with the javelin. In his leisure time he went hunting.

In the following years, Julius Caesar became master of Rome and her colonies. And in 47 B.C. he made Antipater ruler of Palestine. In turn, Antipater made his eldest son, Phasael, governor of Jerusalem and Herod the ruler of Galilee. Thus, Herod was in politics. And he had started near the top.

About this time, Herod met Mark Antony at Petra and they formed a lifelong friendship. But it was a friendship that nearly destroyed Herod.

Always conscious that he was only a commoner and not even a racial Jew, Herod wished he could hide his origins from the public. This, of course, was impossible.

Herod the Great

But there was a way to help his personal cause. If he could marry into the highest circles, the glow of his wife would shield him. And so he began to look around. Soon his eyes fell on the exquisitely beautiful Mariamne.

Mariamne was the granddaughter of John Hyrcanus II, a Maccabean—and the present high priest! The Maccabees had won the nation a former independence from the Seleucids, and thus being related to them would be a dazzling honor. Forthwith, he divorced his wife Doris, an Edomite like himself, and went after Mariamne. With his considerable charm, they were soon engaged. The heights were still in the distance, but he was in the foothills—and was climbing.

And then in 44 B.C. the peace of the world was shattered by the murder of Julius Caesar in the Roman Senate on the Ides (fifteenth) of March. Mark Antony was confident that Caesar had named him the new ruler. He was mistaken. According to the will, the new master of Rome was to be Caesar's grandnephew—eighteen-year-old Octavian!

Judea was shocked by Caesar's death. Suetonius wrote: "Public grief was enhanced by crowds of foreigners lamenting in their fashion, especially Jews who loved Caesar for the friendship he had shown them." Julius Caesar had exempted Jews from military service; had allowed them to send money to the Temple; and had restored to them the vital port of Joppa.

Antony and Octavian joined forces to defeat the assassins—Brutus and Cassius. And in the famous battle of Philippi—where Paul founded the first European church a century later—Antony won the victory and saved Octavian's life. Now with Brutus and Cassius dead, the Triumvirate made up of Octavian, Lepidus, and Antony, took over their previously agreed assignments. Being ruler of the eastern section, Antony sailed up the Orontes River to Antioch.

At his headquarters in the Daphne Park, Antony faced a huge delegation of Jews. After listening patiently to their complaints about Herod, he turned to Hyrcanus.

Herod the Great

"Who are the best rulers?" he demanded.

"Herod and his party," replied the high priest.

Then in Judge Roy Bean style, Antony immediately appointed Herod and his brother Phasael as tetrarchs. The word means *ruler of a fourth*. This meant that they were now official rulers of a part of the territory. Antony also recognized Hyrcanus, the Maccabean, as *ethnark—ruler of the nation*.

Herod left with a light heart. His fortunes were rising; and within a short time Mariamne would be his. Indeed, she might even become a queen. Other troubles, however, were brewing.

By 40 B.C.—only two years after the battle of Philippi—the Parthians, an Indo-European race from what is now Iran—conquered Syria. But these lustful warriors with their frizzed beards were not satisfied with just Syria. Soon they began to covet Jerusalem. Jerusalem, however, had thick walls and fierce defenders. The realistic Parthians knew this, and so they decided on intrigue. And for this purpose, they had an ideal pawn—Antigonus.

Antigonus was a frustrated Hasmonean. (The rule by the Maccabean family was known as the Hasmonean Dynasty.) Along with his father, Aristobulus II, the last of the independent Hasmonean kings, and other members of the royal family, Antigonus was sent as a prisoner to Rome by Pompey after his conquest of Jerusalem in 63 B.C.

Six years later, Antigonus and his father escaped. But soon they were captured and sent back to Rome. After a while, however, he and the other children were allowed to return to Judea. Next, he went to Rome and pled with Julius Caesar to be made king of Judea. Julius Caesar, turned down his request for he preferred Antipater, the father of Herod.

The Parthians approached Antigonus with an attractive offer. If he would cooperate with them, they would put him on the Judean throne in the place of his

Herod the Great

uncle, John Hyrcanus II. Antigonus was delighted with this offer, and responded with a bargaining point of his own: If they succeeded in putting him on the throne, he would give them one thousand talents (over a million dollars) and five hundred highborn women. And among those highborn women, according to Josephus, would be the wives and daughters of Herod and his brothers! Following this sinister agreement, the Parthians began their advance.

Soon Acre fell, and then, filled with confidence, they headed toward Jerusalem. Here, skirmishes and then pitched battles were fought in the streets. At the feast of Pentecost thousands of armed pilgrims pulled out their daggers and helped Antigonus. Hard pressed, Herod lost all the city with the exception of the palace area. At this point the Parthian general persuaded Phasael—Herod's older brother—and Hyrcanus to leave and negotiate with Barzaphranes, the Parthian king, then in Galilee.

Herod feared trickery and advised against going. But Phasael and Hyrcanus would not listen. In Galilee, just as Herod had feared, the men were arrested and loaded with chains. Antigonus then went one step further. His uncle Hyrcanus had been high priest for thirty-six years, and Antigonus felt certain that this was much too long. And so he persuaded the Parthians to snip off his ears and exile him in Babylon. This mutilation served to keep Hyrcanus from being high priest again, for according to Leviticus 21:17, a priest had to be without blemish.

Knowing he couldn't win, Herod, in Jerusalem, assembled his mother, Mariamne and her mother, the five hundred ladies whom Antigonus was going to give away, along with thousands of others. When it was pitch black, he led them through the Dung Gate and out of the city. About nine thousand—some authorities say ten thousand—escaped with him. This escape is hard to explain, for he was guarded by ten Parthian officers and two hundred cavalrymen. Nevertheless, he escaped!

Recently a tetrarch and now a fugitive, Herod's

From his palace on top of the cone-shaped hill now called the Herodion, Herod commanded a view of the approach from all directions.

Herod the Great

arrogance sagged to a new low. When the wagon bearing his mother overturned, he was so shaken he started to commit suicide. But when he learned that she was safe, he changed his mind.

By dawn, the Parthians and Jews discovered his escape and started after him. They caught up with him at a place known now as the Herodion just southeast of Bethlehem, about seven miles from Jerusalem. Knowing they faced slavery if they lost, the men out-performed themselves and routed the enemy. Farther south, five miles beyond Hebron, Herod's men joined those of his younger brother, Joseph. It was here they decided to disband the troops and lodge their families at Masada. Joseph agreed to guard them with eight hundred men.

The Hamonean ruler Jonathan had some years before erected a fortress on this rocky cliff. With keen foresight, Herod saw the advantages of this stronghold and made it a place of refuge complete with storehouses of supplies. Josephus tells the story. "Upon the top of the hill, Jonathan the high priest first of all built a fortress, and called it Masada; after which the rebuilding of this place employed the care of King Herod to a great degree; he also built a wall around the entire top of the hill, seven furlongs long; it was composed of white stones; and its height was twelve and its breadth twelve cubits; there were also erected upon that wall thirty-eight towers, each of them fifty cubits high. . . .

"Moreover, he built a palace therein at the western ascent. . . . Now the wall of the palace was very high and very strong, and had at its four corners towers sixty cubits high. . . . He had also cut many and great pits, as reservoirs of water, out of the rocks. . . ."

Safe in this fortress, Herod tried to get allies. Failing in this, he managed to sail for Rome. There, both Octavian and Antony listened with sympathy. Deeply moved, they presented Herod to the Senate; and the Senate voted him the title King of the Jews. But being voted king, and actually being king were two different matters, for Antigonus was firmly in control.

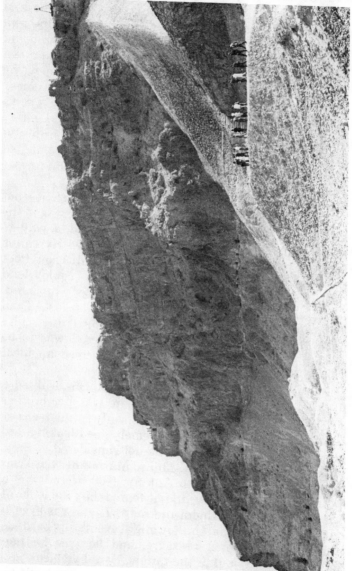

Masada. Visitors today can climb this elevation and explore Herod's remarkable fortress palace built in the first century.

Herod the Great

Herod, however, had his appointment from Rome, and so therefore he summoned the Romans to help—and eventually they came. In the winter of 37 B.C. Herod laid siege to Jerusalem. The trees in the area were cut down and formed into siege engines; and like Pompey, he attacked from the north—a side unprotected by ravines.

In the midst of the siege, Herod solemnized his vows with Mariamne. He needed all the help he could get!

At the end of five months the city fell on a day of fasting. Antigonus was placed in chains and dispatched to Antony in Antioch. There, he was scourged on a cross and later beheaded.

Herod was now thirty-six and was on the throne—but he was not quite supreme. No, the real power was in the hands of the high priest. But Herod had a way to manipulate that office. Cleverly he recalled Hyrcanus from exile. Having been mutilated, Hyrcanus could not be high priest. Still, the old man could lend influence—especially to his granddaughter's husband. Next, he had Ananel, an obscure priest from Mesopotamia, assigned the position. The understanding, of course, was that Herod was to be consulted on all major decisions. It seemed an ideal arrangement.

Mariamne, however, had other ideas! She wanted a high priest in her family—and there was her brother Aristobulus. True, the lad was only seventeen or eighteen. However, he was extremely good looking and according to Leviticus, age was not considered.

Herod did not want him. And so Mariamne went over his head and appealed to Antony. Now Herod was a realist. He knew Antony; and he feared the good looks of the boy might overwhelm the man. There was even a remote possibility that the boy might eventually be made king. But because of pressure, and because he had thought of a way out of the tangle, Herod yielded.

Aristobulus was extremely popular. Dressed in glittering robes, he was a stunning sight. Moreover, he was a Maccabee. Herod watched; ground his teeth, swallowed; forced a smile—and waited.

Herod's time to act came immediately after the Feast of Tabernacles. On an extremely hot day, he led Aristobulus aside during a feast at Jericho. He then suggested a swim. Late in the evening, while the water was covered with shadows, someone held the high priest's head under until he drowned.

Ananel was then returned to office. Herod was now all powerful. He covered the drowning by staging an elaborate funeral. But Mariamne knew; and she refused to forgive her husband.

The ship of state was now moving smoothly again. Herod decided this was the time to settle old scores. For years he had hated the Sanhedrin because when he was ruling in Galilee they had tried him for executing a brigand without first consulting them. He decided the time had come for a purge. Remembering those who had been against him, he had them executed—all forty-five of them! In addition, their entire estates were confiscated. He then nominated another forty-five. This was so the body could have its required seventy-one members.

Herod was now a confident, swaggering dictator. And then unexpectedly his world almost disintegrated. Augustus Caesar—Octavian's new title—declared war on Antony and Cleopatra. Herod immediately threw his weight on the side of Antony. Alas, he guessed wrong! Antony and Cleopatra were so utterly defeated in the sea battle of Actium off the west coast of Greece, they committed suicide.

Terrified by his awkward position, Herod called on Augustus Caesar on the Island of Rhodes. Thoroughly humiliated, the King of the Jews removed his crown and begged for mercy. His only resource was his considerable charm. Smiling bravely, he explained that he had made efforts to get Antony to leave Cleopatra. Augustus listened, and being a practical man, forgave. Herod was bloody. Still, he could handle the troublesome Jews.

Herod the Great

"Put on your crown!" he ordered.

Herod replaced his crown, but he remained an unhappy man. Mariamne was unforgiving. The rift increased. Herod accused her of adultery. Finally, he ordered a trial. Then he had her executed. Now, his personal troubles really began; for Herod really loved Mariamne. Again and again he rushed around his palace calling, "Mariamne! Mariamne!" He fled to the desert for peace, but peace eluded him. On his return he became morbid, sullen. Then a new fear dominated him.

What would he do if a sympathetic public wanted Mariamne's sons to be rulers in his place? And this was a real possibility, for they had royal blood! It was a problem that had to be settled at once. Herod did not hesitate. He ordered them executed.

They were strangled.

Upon hearing of these murders, Augustus Caesar commented, "It is better to be Herod's pig than his son." This remark had grim humor in it, for as a practicing Jew, Herod would not kill a pig!

Sooner than he hoped, Herod began to age. He dyed his hair; took special baths; married new women, including Mariamne II; and went on expensive trips. Nothing satisfied. Thinking the end was close, he made a will which named his son Antipater his successor. This relieved his mind for the moment. Then in his sixty-eighth or sixty-ninth year, the wise men from the east came to Jerusalem. These sages talked about a star and a babe who was to be King of the Jews.

The words of these men from the east so alarmed him, he sent for them. One wonders about his thoughts as he peered into their faces. Did he remember the other wise man, Menahem? Also, the mention of Bethlehem must have revived old memories; for when he escaped from Jerusalem with the nine thousand, it was near this city where he was overtaken.

Such questions cannot be answered. But the New Testament relates that Herod ordered all the children in

Herod the Great

Bethlehem from two years and under to be slaughtered in an attempt to kill the future King of the Jews. History is silent about this episode. Still, it so fits Herod's character we are forced to believe it.

As he neared seventy, Herod lost patience with his son Antipater, had him arrested, and changed his will. Next, he fled to Jericho seeking relief in this tropical resort city from the disease that had gripped him. While peeling an apple, he suddenly raised the blade to stab himself. A stronger hand, however, stopped him.

News of the suicide attempt reached Antipater in the dungeon. Assuming that his father was dead, he tried to get the jailer to release him. Instead, the jailer reported to Herod. In a fit of rage, Herod raised himself on his elbow and ordered his son's immediate execution. He then drew up a new will making his remaining sons rulers. Antipas was to be tetrarch of Galilee and Perea; Archelaus king of Judea, Samaria and Idumea; Philip tetrarch of Gaulonitis, Trachonitis and Paneas. And to his sister Salome he left some cash, some groves, and two cities.

Four days later, suffering from lack of breath, a gangrenous and maggoty scrotum, dreadful itching, malfunction of the kidneys, ulceration of the bowels, and many other things, he died. He died on March 13, 4 B.C. The date is accurate because on that night there was an eclipse of the moon as mentioned by Josephus. (This proves that Jesus was born before the year 1 B.C., for Herod was alive during Jesus' first years.) Archelaus provided an elaborate funeral. The masses attended. But it was hard for them to weep!

The career of Herod the Great was summed up well by Joseph Klausner. Said he: "He stole to the throne like a fox, ruled like a tiger, and died like a dog."

Augustus Caesar approved the will. And thus, those who were given power to rule, received it. Unfortunately, many of the acts of the heirs were evil and cruel. Today, these descendants of Herod are remembered mostly because of the early Christians they tried to eliminate.

26

CHAPTER 2

Augustus, the Teen-Age Emperor

In describing the birth of Christ, Luke wrote: "And it came to pass in those days, that there went out a decree from Caesar Augustus, that all the world should be taxed" (Luke: 2:1). By that simple statement, he pinpointed the date; for all civilization knew about Augustus Caesar!

Indeed, Augustus Caesar, the first emperor of the Roman Empire, was one of the most colorful men who ever lived. Crammed within his triangular skull was more ability than that possessed by a handful of ordinary men. According to historians, he stands shoulder to shoulder with Constantine the Great as one of the Empire's most creative rulers. But strangely, Augustus was not his real name; and although Rome knew her greatest glory under him, he started his flamboyant career when he was an awkward teen-ager of eighteen!

As Julius Caesar was dying from the wounds he had received in the Roman Senate in 44 B.C., those who witnessed his assassination wondered who his successor would be. Mark Antony was all but certain that he was the chosen one. But on the 19th of March, when he secured the will from the Vestal Virgins, he was stunned

Augustus Caesar

to learn that Caesar had bequeathed his fortune to his three grandnephews, and that he had named one of them—Caius Octavius—his son and heir!

Antony—known for his gross immorality—had already summoned Caesar's army to Rome. Alarmed by the famous general's power, the Senate hastened to invite young Caius Octavius to Rome. At the time the message arrived, Caius was with the army at Apollonia in Illyria. The lad was shocked at the news of his great-uncle's death. He and Julius had been very close. They had traveled to Spain together, and during the last several years Caius had spent much of his time in the palace at Rome.

As Caius Octavius approached the city on the Tiber, his mother advised him to stay in hiding—warning that Antony would kill him. But although Caius was only eighteen, he was no coward. He went to see Antony and had a heart-to-heart talk with him.

To the boy's horror, he found that Antony was not obeying Julius Caesar's will. Instead, he was raising an army to subdue Brutus who had refused to give up his claim on Cisalpine Gaul. The will had bequeathed three hundred sesterces (a little over one hundred dollars) to every Roman citizen. When Caius suggested that this should be paid, Antony managed one delay after the other. Caius then borrowed the money and paid the legacy to each of Caesar's veterans. Next, he changed his name to Caius Julius Caesar Octavianus and proceeded to raise an army of his own.

Soon the armies met at Mutina—in north central Italy. There was a sharp fight and Octavian's forces won. Octavian then returned to Rome in triumph. Next a compromise was arranged. The Senate voted for a Second Triumverate. Octavian became the ruler of the West; Antony was given Egypt, Greece, and the East; and Lepidus was put in charge of Africa.

But before the three Triumvirs settled down to govern, they decided to eliminate their enemies and confiscate their property. A long list was drawn up. This sinister document included three hundred senators and two thousand business men. The entire list was condemned to death without trial.

"To have money became a capital crime; children to whom fortunes had been left were condemned and killed; widows were shorn of their legacies; 1400 rich women were required to turn over a large share of their property to the Triumvirs; at last even the savings deposited with the Vestal Virgins were seized. . . . The Triumvirs set soldiers to guard all exits from the city. The proscribed hid in wells, sewers, attics, chimneys. . . . Salvius the tribune, knowing himself doomed, gave a last feast to his friends; the emissaries of the Triumvirs entered, cut off his head, left his body at the table, and bade the feast go on. Slaves took the opportunity to get rid of hard masters, but many fought to death to protect their owners; one disguised himself as his master and suffered decapitation in his stead. . . .

"By Antony's command Cicero's right hand was . . . cut off and brought with the head to the Triumvir. Antony laughed in triumph, gave the assassins 250,000 drachmas, and had head and hand hung up in the Forum." (*Caesar and Christ* by Will Durant.)

At the end of the blood bath, the Triumvirs combined their armies and marched through Macedonia and Thrace where they sought a confrontation with the forces of Brutus and Cassius—the assassins of Julius Caesar.

But even as the Triumvirs marched, Cassius and Brutus were busy strengthening their armies. In desperate need of funds to pay their troops, they forced the cities in the Eastern Empire to pay their taxes ten years in advance. Cassius sent his soldiers to Tarsus, where Paul was to be born some years later. He placed them in the homes of the citizens and vowed that they would not leave until what is equal to $9,000,000 had been raised. And in order to obtain this money, municipal lands were sold at auction; boys and girls and later older people were made into slaves; and the temple vessels were melted down for their precious metal.

Cassius also went into Judea. There, he demanded an amount equal to $4,200,000. And since the cash was not available, he sold the entire population of four towns into slavery.

Finally, in September 42 B.C., the rival armies met on the plains just below Philippi—the city where the jailer was converted. The Triumvirs were successful; and Cassius asked his shield-bearer to kill him and the man obeyed. Brutus, also, took his own life by throwing himself on his sword.

One would think that this would be the end of the fighting. Not so; for now Antony and Octavian faced each other. Antony had married Octavian's sister and had lived with her until he fell for the charms of Cleopatra and began to have children by her.

The dispute between these brothers-in-law came to a flaming end on September 2, 31 B.C., when the two met in a gigantic sea battle at Actium—just off the western coast of Greece. Octavian's men managed to set fire to Antony and Cleopatra's ships. An ancient writer described the holocaust. "Some sailors perished by the smoke before the flames reached them; others were roasted in their vessels as though in ovens. Many leaped into the sea. . . . "

Between them, Antony and Cleopatra had 500 ships. Nonetheless, they lost and fled. Later, they both committed suicide—she, by allowing an asp to bite her breast; and he, by thrusting a dagger into himself.

Octavian was now master of the world and the Mediterranean had become a Roman lake. He even controlled the Roman colonies in Africa for Lepidus had retired. With his new power, Octavian proceeded to put the Empire in order. He stopped piracy which had been running wild, punished corrupt officials, and established a firm government of law and order. While doing this, he raided the treasury of Egypt and brought the money to Rome. This provided such an overabundance of money that interest rates fell from twelve to four percent and the value of real estate soared.

Next, he reorganized the government and had himself named *princeps senatus* which roughly means "first on the roll call of the Senate."

With his firm hand, money came out of hiding and an abundant prosperity settled over the entire Empire. The Senate was so thankful for his success they gave him the title *Augustus*. The title comes from the word *augere* which means to increase. Formerly it was only used in connection with holy objects.

What kind of a man was this Augustus who ruled so serenely while Jesus was spending His youthful years in Nazareth? History informs us that he had sandy hair, merging brows, an odd-shaped head, and penetrating eyes. He suffered from a kind of ringworm that caused his skin to itch; had gallstones; and was so sensitive to the cold that in winter he wore "a woolen chest protector, wraps for his thighs and shins, an undershirt, four tunics (blouses), and a heavy toga."

Also, a form of rheumatism had so crippled his left leg he walked with a slight limp. He could not ride horseback long, tired easily, and his right hand frequently became stiff with what might have been arthritis. These and other problems made him a near-invalid. But he managed to survive, for he was scrupulously careful with his diet. He insisted on only the plainest foods. A typical meal consisted of a little fish, cheese, coarse bread, and fruit. Often he ate alone—especially before a banquet. Thus he had an excuse not to eat the rich foods that were being served.

Usually he treated his illnesses with home remedies; but when a doctor cured him of a serious disease, he was so thankful he decreed that all doctors in the Empire were exempt from taxation! One wonders if this ruling was still in effect in the days of Luke.

Augustus Caesar

Augustus was superstitious. He carried a sealskin to protect himself from lightning and he was very careful about his activities during "unlucky" days. Modesty, he believed, was a virtue. He lived in a gaudy age. Still, he refused to succumb to its lure. He wore clothes woven by the women of the palace and insisted on sleeping in a tiny room dubbed the *cubiculum*.

About the time Jesus was being taken by His parents to the Temple in Jerusalem, a revolt against Roman authority was organized in Germany. The Roman governor Varus was lured into a trap beyond the Rhine and he along with three legions were utterly destroyed. When Augustus was informed of the disaster, he was so shaken he refused to shave or cut his hair for months. And sometimes he repeatedly dashed his head against the wall while he wailed: "Quintilius Varus, give me back my legions!"

Oddly enough, one of Rome's problems was that of a lowering birthrate among its citizens. Large families became decidedly unpopular and so the practice of infanticide became widespread. Infants were left out in the cold to perish. At the same time people were freeing their slaves because they were too poor to feed them; and since the state supplied free food to all freedmen, the state had to look after them. In addition, many slaves were buying their freedom.

Augustus became alarmed over the situation. He feared that the racial stock of Rome was changing. In order to stop this, he had a series of unique laws passed. One of these decreed that the owner of two slaves might free both of them; but the owner of from three to ten slaves could only free half of them; and no one was allowed to free more than one hundred slaves.

Also, he tried to encourage Romans to have more children. A lady worth more than 20,000 sesterces was required to pay a one percent tax on her wealth each year. But this tax was reduced on the birth of each child, and after the third child it was eliminated completely.

Augustus Caesar

Augustus denounced racial suicide and made lavish gifts to many who raised large families. When a slave had quintuplets, he had a monument raised in her honor.

Augustus was horrified at the lowering of the moral standard, even though his own morals were extremely questionable. He decreed that teen-agers could not go to public entertainments unless they were accompanied by an adult relative. Women were not allowed at athletic contests, and were restricted to the upper seats at gladiatorial fights.

The emperor who started to rule the Empire as a teenager continued to rule until his death in A.D. 14. At that time he was seventy-six. His life overflowed with crime; but he had a steady hand. Without knowing it, he helped make way for the spread of Christianity. He did this by strengthening the postal system, establishing a vast network of roads, and by keeping a relative peace throughout the world.

As he was dying, he quoted the last lines from a Roman comedy: "Since well I've played my part, clap now your hands, and with applause dismiss me from the stage." He then embraced his third wife, Livia; bade her farewell, and was gone.

His body was cremated on the Field of Mars.

CHAPTER 3

Mama's Boy, Tiberius Caesar

Some called him "Mud-and-Blood"; others "The Old Goat." And when he died many Romans were so relieved they risked their lives by shouting: "To the Tiber with Tiberius!" Nevertheless, this mama's boy ruled the Roman Empire from A.D. 14-37. And since this rule, like a shadow, extended across the ministry of John the Baptist, the Resurrection of Jesus Christ, and the conversion of Paul, the story of Tiberius Caesar is extremely important.

Indeed, the fact that Christianity could be born and flower with such a monster on the throne, is one of the proofs of the vitality of the gospel!

When the disciples handled coins with the image of Tiberius on them, they saw a tall, broad-shouldered man with fine, deep-set eyes. Tiberius wore his hair low over the nape of his neck, and he was so strong he could "poke a finger through a sound, newly-plucked apple" declared Suetonius. And yet he was shy and miserable because of acne!

Few killed others with as little reason as Tiberius. Thousands were executed during his reign. He signed death warrants with the same carelessness with which

Tiberius

he ate his food. And yet he was so dominated by his mother he allowed her to co-sign many of his imperial decrees!

Tiberius was the first of the Claudian dynasty which ended with the Nero who executed Paul. He became emperor only through chance, and a slight one at that. At the time of the birth of Jesus, Augustus Caesar was on the throne. Soon the roving eye of Augustus fell on Livia, the wife of Nero—a former admiral of Julius Caesar's fleet. At the time, Livia had already borne one child to Nero and another was on the way. Such trivialities, however, did not matter to the great Augustus. He insisted that she marry him immediately; and this she did even though it so crushed Nero he died shortly afterwards.

Livia's first child was Tiberius and thus Augustus became his stepfather. Tiberius had the most aristocratic blood in Italy. Both parents were Claudians—and the Claudians were from the top of the top drawer. This haughty clan liked to trace their ancestors right back to the founding of Rome. And so with this kind of blood and the influence of Augustus, the future of Tiberius was assured. This is so even though Augustus was not particularly fond of him.

Tiberius attended the finest schools and acquired an excellent education. And yet he was not happy because he was constantly being ordered about by his mother—and Augustus. In his youth he met the lovely Vipsania, daughter of another admiral, Marcus Agrippa. Both Tiberius and Vipsania enjoyed the sea. Soon they were married and were extremely happy. Then Augustus got another family-shattering idea.

Augustus had had three wives: Claudia, Scribonia, and Livia. But like Solomon, he had only one child, a daughter by Scribonia. This daughter, Julia, was the apple of his eye. When she was only fourteen, Augustus persuaded his sister Octavia to insist that her son Marcellus divorce his wife and marry Julia. Two years later Marcellus died and the attractive widow became the scandal of Rome. Augustus then forced forty-two-year-old Agrippa to divorce his wife and marry her.

Following Agrippa's death, Augustus decreed that Tiberius break with Vipsania and marry Julia. Tiberius did not want to do this for he was deeply attached to Vipsania—moreover Vipsania was pregnant. But Augustus had spoken and so Tiberius did what he was told. And this was to his sorrow, for Julia continued to have affairs with other men.

Soon, however, Augustus himself got disgusted with Julia. At a gay party, he astonished the guests by announcing that she had been banished to "a barren rock off the Campanian coast." But the damage to Tiberius—damage that he would avenge by killing his thousands—had already been done.

While Augustus was dying in A.D. 14, he realized that Tiberius was going to succeed him. He had already paved the way for this event by legally adopting him as his son. Still, Augustus was unhappy. As the attendants waited at the royal bed, he gasped: "Poor Rome, doomed to be masticated by those slow-moving jaws!"

Yes, Tiberius was slow of speech; but his mind was like a trap. He had carefully planned his future and he knew exactly what he was going to do. At first he pretended that he really didn't want the power of an emperor. He declared that he would much rather work with a number of rulers. But the Senate was not deceived. Said one courageous senator: "Some people are slow to do what they promise; you are slow to promise what you have already done."

Finally, and with fake reluctance, Tiberius agreed to become the new emperor. Even then, he made a subtle suggestion that he might resign at a later date! And since he was already 55, many believed that the date of his resignation was just a short time away. Soon the Senate began to vote him honors. But on each occasion he vetoed the bill; and this brought more honors.

Tiberius

Tiberius never remarried and his mother took advantage of this by moving in with him. In the palace, she practically told him what to do; and she felt she had a right to do this, for she had paved the way to his success. Dio, a Roman biographer, says: "But not satisfied to rule on equal terms with him, she wished to assert a superiority over him . . . and undertook to manage everything like a sole ruler." As a dutiful son, he listened—and obeyed. But as he grew into his sixties his mother became intolerable. In desperation, he moved her into a separate house.

Like other Romans, Tiberius was superstitious and believed in omens. This tendency was a natural one for his mother was always listening to astrologers and using other means to discover the future. "Just before his (Tiberius') birth," wrote Suetonius, "Livia had tried various means of foretelling whether her child would be male or female; one was to take an egg from underneath a broody hen and warm it alternately in her own hands and in those of her women—and she successfully hatched a cock-chick which already had a fine comb."

Tiberius believed in astrology; and like many who have a weakness of which they are ashamed, he soothed his conscience by persecuting others. All astrologers were banned from Rome unless they agreed to make no more predictions. Those who disobeyed were sold into slavery. Likewise, he banished all foreign religions—especially those of Egypt and all forms of Judaism. And when a Jewish youth was of military age he was sent to a camp in an unhealthy region, the hope being that he would acquire a fatal disease.

All of his laws were not damaging. He fought crime by increasing the police force; and he kept gladiator duels to a minimum. Tiberius was extremely economical with the public treasury. Foreign dignitaries were often shocked by his economies. Often at banquets—even the best—he served leftovers! If one side of a boar had been served one day, he saw no reason why the other side should not be served the next. At the time he took office there were one hundred million sesterces in the Treasury. By the end of his rule there were almost three billion sesterces in the accounts.

On the surface, Tiberius appeared a humble man. When bills were presented in the Senate which would change the names of the months of September and October to Tiberius and Livius in honor of himself and his mother, he refused to have anything to do with them. "What would you do should there be thirteen Caesars?" he demanded. But beneath that smooth surface he was cunning, cruel, grasping.

As the affairs of Rome started to improve, the private life of Tiberius began to disintegrate. In his 67th year he moved to the Island of Capri and began a life of utter debauchery that is probably unexcelled in history. Luke tells us that John the Baptist was preaching in the wilderness during "the fifteenth year of Tiberius Caesar" (Luke 3:1). He also tells us that Jesus was baptized during this period when He "began to be about thirty years of age" (3:23). And so as Jesus was gathering His disciples, healing the sick, and then dying on the cross, the leader of the Roman Empire—an old man in his seventies—was giving himself to unnatural vice.

Under his leadership, Capri became such a wicked place it was sneered at as "Caprineum." The palace was filled with lewd pictures and statues; and the vilest type of pornography was brought to him. His wickedness was so gross and so continuous—(it especially involved children)—that it is far too revolting to write about. All that can be said is that his mind was as corrupt as a sewer.

Tiberius felt especially inspired to protect the name of Augustus. When a man was accused of removing the head from a statue of his stepfather, he ordered the man executed. This lust to kill increased with his age. Suetonius makes the almost unbelievable remark that "People could now be executed for beating a slave or

Tiberius

Ruins of Forum of Augustus Caesar. Even today one can still view a memorial to Augustus Caesar in Rome.

changing their clothes close to an image of Augustus, or for carrying a ring or coin bearing Augustus' head into a privy. . . . The climax came when a man died merely for letting an honor be voted him by the native town council on the same day that honors had once been voted to Augustus."

Tiberius was so corrupt that talented men wrote poems about him. One which must have been scrawled in many a back alley had this verse:

> *He is not thirsty for neat wine*
> *As he was thirsty then,*
> *But warms him up a tastier cup—*
> *The blood of murdered men.*

At the time of the resurrection of Jesus Christ, someone asked Tiberius what he thought about it; and he was alleged to have replied that he didn't believe it, for the Senate had not voted on whether or not Jesus was divine!

A few days before his death, the Capri lighthouse collapsed during an earthquake. Superstitious Tiberius felt certain that this was an omen indicating that he was near the end. From then on, he was troubled by dreadful dreams.

Death finally came in his seventy-ninth year. The details of his passing are wrapped in mystery. But since those details are closely connected with the career of his successor, Caligula, we will leave them for the next chapter.

CHAPTER 4

Caligula, the Tyrant

One of Caligula's best friends was Herod Agrippa, the impulsive nephew of the Herod before whom Jesus stood on the day of His trial.

Herod was twenty years older than the teen-age Caligula. But instead of being a barrier, this span of years merely enabled the older one to pass on the knowledge of more vice. Moreover, Caligula was a zealous student!

While the two were enjoying a chariot ride, the conversation drifted onto the subject of what Caligula would do after he had inherited the throne. Knowing that Tiberius would be merciless to anyone who longed for his death, the two friends spoke in whispers. Unfortunately for himself, Herod was carried away with enthusiasm.

Speaking a little too loudly, Herod suggested that after the death of Tiberius, it would be easy to take care of Gemellus. The driver overheard the remark and repeated it to the Emperor. Tiberius immediately ordered Herod's arrest. Some time later, in the spring of A.D. 37, an old friend visited Herod in prison. Speaking in Hebrew, he whispered in his ear, "The old lion is dead."

Overjoyed, Herod ordered a feast to which he invited all the prison officials. But just as they started to gorge,

Caligula

word came that Tiberius wasn't dead after all. The "guests" responded by shoving away all the dishes and binding their flabbergasted host in chains!

The report, however, was merely an exaggeration. Although still alive, Tiberius was on his deathbed. And as he rolled and tossed, he prayed to his gods for direction in choosing a new emperor. Finally he decided that he would summon both Caligula and Gemellus to his bedside in the morning, and that the one who arrived first would receive the throne.

Curiously, Gemellus overslept and dallied at his breakfast. Thus, Caligula arrived first at the royal bedside. Tiberius was furious, for he distrusted Caligula.

Caligula was tall, slender, had thin hair on his head, and his tight little mouth was inclined to open to one side. He had heavy brows, unblinking eyes; and sometimes when he spoke the words slipped out in a snarl.

But since Caligula was the first to his side, Tiberius had no alternative but to make him the new emperor. A few minutes later the old man closed his eyes, and it was thought that he was dead. Soon the room was packed with well-wishers. But just as they were congratulating him, Tiberius sat up and demanded something to eat.

Caligula was terrified. He feared his great uncle might have witnessed his unspeakable joy and changed his mind. The courtiers, too, were uneasy, for they knew that one twitch of those powerful lips could send them to their deaths. Slowly, one by one, they slipped into the corridor and hid in other rooms.

But Caligula was not one to risk his future on the whims of a dying man. He grabbed at the Emperor's signet ring. If he could only slip this on his finger, it would symbolize the transfer of power! But Tiberius clenched his fist and would not let him have it. Exactly what followed, no one knows. But it is surmised by a number of authorities that Caligula smothered him—perhaps by ordering the blankets over his head, or with a pillow.

Caligula

The moment Tiberius was clearly dead, Caligula gave his first official order. And that was that the servant who had witnessed the old man's death be executed at once.

And thus Caligula became the ruler of the Roman Empire!

Caligula, however, was not his real name. His real name was Gaius Caesar Augustus Germanicus. The nickname Caligula—Little Boot—was given him by the soldiers because when he was young he dressed as an enlisted man and wore *caligae*—soldier's boots. His grandmother on his father's side was a daughter of Antony; and his grandmother on his mother's side was the daughter of Augustus. With these two conflicting streams in his veins, and with the descendants of these two rival families about him, Caligula was as taut as the string of a bow.

During the first seven months of his reign, Caligula was a model of moderation. He assured the Senate that he would listen to them—that he was their servant. He gave great public banquets and was generous with his opposition. But during late autumn he became dangerously ill. On his recovery, he was a different man.

Soon he fell in love with his own sister Drusilla. Since she was already married, he forced her to leave her husband and marry him. He then told the shocked Roman society that this was perfectly all right, and that no one should complain. He argued that the Pharaohs had done this and since Rome ruled Egypt it was perfectly legal for him.

This argument did not convince his grandmother, Antonia; and since she refused to keep silent, he ordered her to poison herself. He then had her cremated in front of his dining room window. As the smoke curled up before him, he shrugged.

About this time Gemellus came to dinner smelling of cough medicine. Caligula instantly accused him of having taken an antidote to protect himself from poison; and since this reflected on him, he ordered Gemellus to

Caligula

commit suicide. The eighteen-year-old youth complied by falling on his sword.

Ordering people to kill themselves now became a hobby with Caligula. Again and again he ordered all sorts of people in many strata of society to take their own lives. And each time, as they obeyed, Caligula's sense of divinity increased. When sitting at dinner with a number of friends, he suddenly burst out laughing. On being asked the reason for his mirth, he replied: "I was just thinking that by a single nod of my head I could have all of your throats cut!" The remark had a sobering effect.

While he embraced either his wife or the lady of his momentary fancy, he liked to remark: "Off comes this beautiful head whenever I give the word."

Caligula's contempt for the masses was complete. And in order to dramatize this contempt, he officially announced that his favorite horse, Incitatus, was a consul. Moreover, he assigned an impressive house and a retinue of servants to the horse. Parties were thrown for distinguished guests with the horse acting as host. These extremes, however, did not satisfy his twisted sense of humor; and so he assigned the horse to a temple and made him a priest!

Always fond of the exotic, he reversed the orders of Tiberius and made the worship of the Egyptian goddess Isis one of the legal cults of Rome. Having no doubts about his rights to satisfy every whim, he filled his life with debauchery. While attending the wedding of a friend, he decided that he should have the bride himself; and so he insisted on marrying her while the groom stood by in speechless astonishment. Then tiring of her, he obtained a divorce.

Caligula loved auctions so much he frequently mounted the table and assumed the role of auctioneer. He especially loved to sell slaves and gladiators; and sometimes he forced the rich to attend his sales. On one occasion, a certain aristocrat who had been forced to attend, nodded in sleep. Caligula interpreted each nod as

Caligula

a bid. When the unfortunate man awakened, he found he had purchased thirteen gladiators for the enormous sum of 9,000,000 sesterces.

Deciding the ordinary water was not good enough for his bath, he bathed in perfume; and he spent 10,000,000 sesterces on a single banquet. This kind of extravagance soon exhausted the ample treasury left by Tiberius. In order to raise more revenue, Caligula taxed almost everything. When this did not bring in sufficient funds, he had rich men condemned for treason and then confiscated their estates. The executioners who led these victims to their deaths were instructed to kill them "by numerous slight wounds, so that they will feel that they are dying."

According to Suetonius, when a meat shortage developed in the zoo, Caligula decreed that all "bald-headed prisoners" be fed to the animals. This was to keep the various beasts in good health. But we must remember that Suetonius was a gossip, and maybe this is mere gossip!

At the beginning of his spectacular career, Caligula announced that he was a god, fully equal to Jupiter. He then ordered the heads on the statues of the gods to be removed and to be replaced with replicas of his own head. Next, he had a thunder machine constructed, and answered "Jove's thunder" with his own, peal for peal. But sometimes the natural thunder was too much for him. On such occasions he crawled whimpering under the bed!

Many of the countries ruled by Caligula found no difficulty in worshiping him, for they already had many gods and it was easy to add another. The Jews, however, refused to worship anyone other than Jehovah. This uncompromising stand brought a lot of persecution down on their heads. Because of this, Philo of Alexandria headed a deputation to see the Emperor.

Philo and his colleagues tried to explain their position to Caligula. But he refused to listen to them seriously.

Caligula

Nevertheless, because of Caligula's friendship with Herod Agrippa, he did not persecute them. However, in order to tease them, he ordered his statue placed in the Holy of Holies in Jerusalem!

This order was never obeyed because of a tidal wave of disapproval from the Jews; but it did provide Caligula with many a light moment.

By the time he was 29, Caligula was an old man. His excesses had drained his vitality; and he was hated by almost the entire Roman Empire. On January 24, A.D. 41, he made the mistake of insulting an officer in his bodyguard once too often. This officer, Cassius Chaerea, yanked out his sword and slashed the Emperor on his shoulder. Then, stunned by what he had done, Chaerea stood to one side and stared.

It seemed impossible that he could have done such a thing.

But as he stared, other members of the guard swooped down on the tyrant and finished him off with their swords.

And thus ended the career of Caligula. Looking back, most historians are agreed that he was insane.

CHAPTER 5

The Descendants of Herod

Altogether, including Herod the Great, seven Herods appear in the New Testament. But since their dramatic intrigues and erratic behavior are so complicated, we do not have space to write about them in depth. Instead, we will sketch their lives in proportion to their importance.

Herod Antipas

Herod Antipas—referred to as Herod in the New Testament—was the son of Herod the Great and Malthace, a Samaritan wife. This means that he had even less Jewish blood than his father! In spite of this, Antipas is mentioned more often in the New Testament than any other Herod. And so sordid was his character, the Pharisees warned Jesus that Antipas sought to kill Him. Jesus responded dubbing him "that fox" (Luke 13:31,32).

According to his father's last will, Antipas was made tetrarch of Galilee. He was never popular and his prestige sank to a new low when he married his niece Herodias, the former wife of his half brother, Philip—son of Cleopatra. (Herodias was the daughter of another half-brother, Aristobulus.)

This double-sin had inspired John the Baptist to

The Herods

reprimand him face to face (Matthew 14:1-4). Later, when Salome, daughter of Herodias by Philip, danced before Antipas, he was so drunk with desire he impulsively agreed to give Herodias anything she wished. His wife's request was immediate. She demanded the head of John the Baptist on a tray. Moreover, although Herod regretted his rash promise, he complied at once.

Herod Antipas is also the Herod to whom Pilate sent Jesus during His trial. Luke has given us a graphic picture of their confrontation. "And when Herod saw Jesus, he was exceeding glad: for he was desirous to see him for a long season, because he had heard many things of him; and he hoped to see some miracles done by him" (Luke 23:8).

Following his one-way conversation with Jesus—it was one-way because Jesus refused to answer—"Herod with his men of war set him at nought, and mocked him, and arrayed him in a gorgeous robe, and sent him again to Pilate" (verse 11).

Like his father, Antipas was an enthusiastic builder. He continued many of the projects his father had started; and he built a new seaport on the southwest shore of Galilee and named it Tiberias in honor of the Roman emperor. He also rebuilt Sepphoris some four miles north of Nazareth—a place where Jesus and Joseph may have worked as carpenters.

Herodias soon became jealous of her half-brother Agrippa I—son of Aristobulus and grandson of Herod the Great and Mariamne I. This was because he had been made king of Judea. In order to advance her husband Antipas, she persuaded him to go with her to Rome and ask Emperor Caligula for a crown. But before they arrived, Agrippa had sent word to Caligula that Antipas was in secret league with the Parthians. Agrippa and Caligula were, or course, old friends; and the youthful emperor chose to believe Agrippa.

Antipas was exiled in A.D. 39. And it is interesting to note that this was only a handful of years after he had

The Herods

mocked Jesus. No one is quite certain as to the place of exile. In one passage Josephus says that it was in Gaul, and in another passage he states that it was in Spain. Herodias shared his exile.

Agrippa I

It is said that Agrippa I—commonly called King Agrippa—was seen standing and weeping in the synagogue. Why? Because he had just read Deuteronomy 17:15. That pivotal passage says: "Thou shalt in any wise set him king over thee, whom the Lord God shall choose: one from among the brethren shalt thou set king over thee: *thou mayest not set a stranger over thee, which is not thy brother* " (italics added).

Agrippa was deeply concerned over the fact that his grandfather, Herod the Great, was not a real Jew. Experts in the Scripture, however, comforted him by pointing out that his grandmother Mariamne was as blue-blooded a Jew as one could find, for she was the granddaughter of the great John Hyrcanus! They also pointed out that a child always takes the nationality of the mother.

Perhaps it was this conflict in his heart that made Agrippa so cruel. He is the one who put James the son of Zebedee to death. When he saw that this pleased the Jews, he arrested Peter and would have done the same to him except for his escape (Acts 12:1-16).

Having gone to school in Rome, and having been a close friend of Caligula, he was inclined to be conceited. His death came as suddenly as the death he had meted out to James. Here is Luke's description: "And upon a set day Herod, arrayed in royal apparel, sat upon his throne, and made an oration unto them. And the people gave a shout, saying, It is the voice of a god, and not a man. And immediately the angel of the Lord smote him, because he gave not God the glory: and he was eaten of worms, and gave up the ghost" (Acts 12:21-23).

Josephus confirms this painful death and adds that he

The Herods

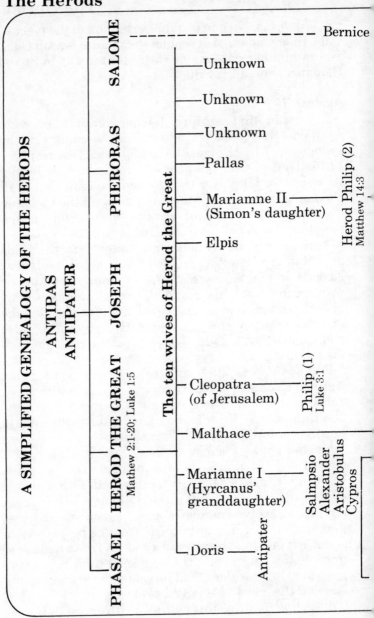

A SIMPLIFIED GENEALOGY OF THE HERODS

PHASAEL

HEROD THE GREAT
Mathew 2:1-20; Luke 1:5

JOSEPH

PHERORAS

SALOME

ANTIPAS
ANTIPATER

Bernice

The ten wives of Herod the Great

- Unknown
- Unknown
- Unknown
- Pallas
- Mariamne II —— Herod Philip (2)
  (Simon's daughter)   Matthew 14:3
- Elpis
- Cleopatra —— Philip (1)
  (of Jerusalem)   Luke 3:1
- Malthace
- Mariamne I —— Salmpsio
  (Hyrcanus'   Alexander
  granddaughter)   Aristobulus
     Cypros
- Doris —— Antipater

52

```
Antipas (1) ———————— Herodias (3)
Luke 3:1                 Mark 6:17-28
Matthew 14:1f            Matthew 14:3-11
Luke 13:31f
Mark 8:15                    Salome (4)
Luke 23:7-12                 Mark 6:22-28
Acts 4:27


                  Agrippa (1)
                    Acts 12

        Agrippa II (5) |  Drusilla (7)
        Acts 25:13; 26:32  Acts 24:24
        Bernice (6)        Drusus
        Acts 25:13; 26:30  Mariamne III?
```

A dotted line indicates marriage; a continuous line, descent.
(1) Recipients of territory in the will of Herod the Great.
(2) Also called Philip of Rome.
(3) Was married to Herod Philip and then to half-brother Antipas.
(4) The one who danced before Antipas, married her uncle, Philip.
(5) Paul appeared before him in the presence of his sister Bernice (Acts 25:23). His relations with his sister Bernice were an open scandal (Acts 25:13,14). He said to Paul, "Almost thou persuadest me to be a Christian" (Acts 26:28).
(6) She became the mistress of Titus who destroyed Jerusalem in A.D. 70.
(7) Wife of Felix, procurator of Judea A.D. 50-60 (Acts 24:24).

The Herods

died in his fifty-fourth year.

Agrippa II

This Herod was the son of Agrippa I, and a full brother to Bernice and Drusilla. Herod the Great was his grandfather. New Testament readers are well acquainted with this Agrippa, for he is the one before whom Paul presented his case at Caesarea.

Luke reports the beginning of this encounter in Acts 25:23. "And on the morrow, when Agrippa was come, and Bernice, with great pomp, and was entered into the place of hearing, with the chief captains, and principal men of the city, at Festus' commandment Paul was brought forth."

Paul had respect for Agrippa's knowledge of the Jews. Said he: "I know thee to be expert in all customs and questions which are among the Jews: wherefore I beseech thee to hear me patiently" (26:30).

The courtroom that day must have been extremely tense, and many of the eyes were certainly focused on Bernice. Although the name Bernice means "bearer of victory," this sister of King Agrippa, or Herod Agrippa as he was also called, was a very wicked woman. She was married twice, was suspected of living incestuously with Agrippa, and later, she became a mistress to Titus in Rome and openly lived with him in the palace.

In his defense, Paul outlined the story of his conversion. In this outline, he exclaimed: "Whereupon, O king Agrippa, I was not disobedient unto the heavenly vision" (Acts 26:19).

One can imagine the intensity with which the court listened to this dynamic man of Tarsus. As he summed up his plea, Paul became very bold and said: "King Agrippa, believest thou the prophets? I know that thou believest" (verse 27). To this trust, Agrippa replied—perhaps sarcastically: "Almost thou persuadest me to be a Christian" (verse 28).

Agrippa was living in Rome at the time of his father's

death in A.D. 44. At the time, he was a mere youth of 17; and the Roman Emperor Claudius felt that he was too young to accept his father's throne. Accordingly, he remained in Rome. Then in A.D. 48 when his uncle, king of Chalcis died, Claudius gave him this throne on the western slope of Anti-Lebanon.

Agrippa II seems to have pleased Claudius and he thus transferred him to the former tetrarchy of Philip which contained Batanea, Trachonitis, and Gaulonitis. And later even more territory was put under his jurisdiction.

As war threatened between Judea and Rome, Agrippa tried to persuade the Jews not to fight. Unsuccessful in this, he fought on the Roman side with Vespasian. He was wounded at the siege of Gamala.

Following the destruction of Jerusalem in A.D. 70, Agrippa and Bernice moved to Rome. There, he was made a praetor. He died in A.D. 100.

Of the statements of Agrippa II which are recorded in Acts, he is especially remembered for his conclusion in regard to Paul. Said he: "This man might have been set at liberty, if he had not appealed to Caesar" (Acts 26:32).

Herod Archelaus

This Herod was the son of Herod the Great and Malthace—and thus a full brother to Herod Antipas. According to his father's will he was made Ethnarch of Judea, Samaria, and Idumea.

This Herod appears in one of the nativity events. Having fled to Egypt with the infant Jesus, Joseph and Mary were returning home after the death of Herod the Great. "But when he [Joseph] heard that Archelaus did reign in Judea in the room of his father Herod, he was afraid to go thither: notwithstanding, being warned of God in a dream, he turned aside into the parts of Galilee" (Matthew 2:22).

Archelaus was in serious trouble with the Jews from the beginning of his reign. Like other Herods, he was morally corrupt. He married Glaphyra, a former wife of

The Herods

RULERS SPANNING NEW TESTAMENT ERA

ROMAN EMPERORS

NAME	RULED	MANNER OF DEATH
Julius Caesar	49—44 B.C.[1]	Stabbed
Augustus Caesar	27 B.C.—A.D. 14[2]	Natural death
Tiberius Caesar	A.D. 14—37	Smothered?
Caligula	A.D. 37—41	Stabbed
Claudius	A.D. 41—54	Poisoned
Nero	A.D. 54—68	Suicide
Galba	A.D. 68	Beheaded
Otho	A.D. 68	Suicide
Vitellius	A.D. 69	Tortured
Vespasian	A.D. 70—79	Natural death
Titus	A.D. 79—81	Natural death
Domitian	A.D. 81—96	Stabbed
Nerva	A.D. 96—98	Natural death
Trajan	A.D. 98—117	Natural death
Hadrian	A.D. 117—138	Suicide?[3]

[1]The year he was made dictator. [2]Following the assassination of Julius Caesar, the Second Triumvirate made up of Augustus (Octavian), Antony and Lepidus shared the rule. Following a civil war, Octavian and Antony defeated Brutus and Cassius the assassins of Julius Caesar. Next, Octavian defeated Antony and Cleopatra. In 31 B.C., Octavian was supreme. But he was not voted the title Augustus until 27 B.C. [3]Hadrian deliberately ate foods he knew would eventually kill him.

RULERS, GOVERNORS, AND PROCURATORS

NAME	RULED	MANNER OF DEMISE
Herod the Great	37 B.C.—4 B.C.[1]	Natural death[2]
Herod Antipas	4 B.C.—A.D. 39	Banished
Herod Archelaus	4 B.C.—A.D. 6	Banished
Herod Agrippa I	A.D. 41—41	Natural death[3]
Herod Agrippa II	A.D. 50—70	Natural death
Philip the Tetrarch	4 B.C.—A.D. 34	Natural death
Pontius Pilate	A.D. 26—37	Suicide? Beheaded?
Felix	A.D. 52—60?	Recalled and saved from punishment by Pallas.
Festus	A.D. ?—62	Died in office.

[1]It is difficult to determine exactly when Herod the Great came into power in Palestine, for he acquired power by degrees. However, the Roman Senate declared him "King of the Jews" just prior to B.C. 37. [2]Herod tried to commit suicide on two occasions. But he died a natural, though dreadful death. [3]His spectacular death is related in Acts 12:20-23. This unusual death is also recorded by Josephus.

his half brother Alexander. And what made this even worse in the eyes of the Jews was that Glaphyra had had three children by Alexander.

Josephus wrote: "But in the tenth year of Archelaus' government, both his brethren and the principal men of Judea and Samaria, not able to bear his barbarous and tyrannical usage of them, accused him before Caesar."

Augustus Caesar responded by exiling him in Gaul. His reign lasted only from 4 B.C. to A.D. 6. But like the other Herods, he dabbled in architecture. He is especially remembered for having rebuilt the royal palace in Jericho.

The exile of Archelaus was a turning point in Jewish history. From this time on the realm was ruled by procurators appointed by Rome.

Philip the Tetrarch

As we have seen, Herod the Great had two wives by the name of Mariamne. Likewise, he had two sons by the name of Philip!

The first Philip was the son of Mariamne II; and the second Philip was the son of Cleopatra. This Philip is called the tetrarch because his father's will made him ruler of Gaulonitis, Trachonitis, and Paneas. His only mention in the Gospels is in Luke 3:1.

This Philip was the founder of the Gentile city, Caesarea Philippi some fifty miles southwest of Damascus. It was at this place where Simon Peter made his famous confession. When Philip died in A.D. 34, the lands he had ruled were assigned to Syria.

Historians rate him as the best of the Herods.

Philip of Rome

This Philip, son of Herod the Great and Mariamne II, is noted for three things. He was the first husband of Herodias who later married Herod Antipas; he was the father of the Salome whose lascivious dance brought about the execution of John the Baptist; and he is also

The Herods

remembered because his father, in a fit of anger, removed his name from his will.

Without lands to rule, Philip lived in Rome and died in obscurity.

CHAPTER 6

Pontius Pilate —He Used a Basin

Although most Christians lump Pontius Pilate together with Judas Iscariot, both Pilate and his wife are devoutly worshiped as saints in Ethiopia. Indeed, June 25 is their feast day. On that occasion, faithful members of the Ethiopic Christian Church are supposed to think *about,* and pray *to* Saint Pilate and his wife!

The reason? Because at the trial of Jesus, Pilate washed his hands and said: "I am innocent of the blood of this just man."

A veil of legend and mystery has been flung around this Roman officer. But there are enough dependable references in secular history and in the New Testament to give us a reasonably definite profile. And so let us flip the centuries back to the Roman year, A.U.C. 784. (A.U.C. stands for *ab urbe condita,* meaning "since the founding of the city." The Roman calendar went back to the mythical founding of Rome by Romulus and Remus in 753 B.C.) On the 15th day of Nisan—Friday, April 7, in the modern calendar—we see Pilate dressed in his Roman toga occupying a regal chair placed on a stone landing near his judgment hall. (We might mention that this date is disputed by those who believe Jesus was

Pontius Pilate

crucified on Wednesday.) A man of fashion, his hair is closely cropped in the Roman way. Defiant guards, their feet astride and a spear in their right hands, stand stiffly on either side. It is about eight o'clock in the morning and Jerusalem is bathed in warm sunshine.

Pilate had reason to be happy. As the fifth procurator of Judea, Samaria, and Idumea, he was a privileged character. (Remember when Herod Archelaus was deposed in A.D. 6, the Romans began to appoint procurators to rule Judea.) Governors of distant provinces in the Roman Empire were not allowed to take their wives along. But an exception had been made with Pilate. Perhaps Claudia had insisted. As the granddaughter of the great Augustus Caesar and the illegitimate daughter of the third wife of Tiberius Caesar, she had influence in Rome!

But this morning Pilate's dark Roman eyes glistened with sullen anger. He was annoyed because of the Jews. Fearing defilement, they refused to come into the regular court as decent and proper men should do. He was also angry because the sight of a Jew—almost any Jew—reminded him of past experiences with them. And this mob brought to mind an experience of a near yesteryear.

Pilate—the name means javelin—was a man who couldn't stand to be different. In every Roman city, with the glaring exception of Jerusalem, images of Caesar were proudly displayed in prominent places. But the Jews would have none of this, for they were so against idolatry even images of Caesar were taboo. And since Tiberius was determined to keep trouble to a minimum, he allowed the Jews to have their way.

This irritated Pilate. He wanted Jerusalem to be like all other cities, and he was determined to have his way—even though he had to resort to trickery. During a dark night, he sent soldiers into Jerusalem and had images of Caesar raised at the fortress Tower of Antonia. The fortress was next to the Temple and thus he knew the

Jews would be incensed. But since this was a fortified area, he reasoned that the Jews would not protest too vigorously for fear of summoning a reprisal from the Romans.

Ah, but Pilate did not know the Jews—not really. Upon the advice of Caiaphas they began to pour into Jerusalem and head for Caesarea, sixty miles away. And as they plodded toward the capital, they gathered followers. By the time they reached Pilate's home, there were seven thousand of them!

But Pilate was unimpressed with numbers. When asked to remove the images he flatly refused. The Jews, however, could be obstinate. They just camped at his door and prayed that God would change his mind.

Every time Pilate looked out the window he saw Jews. Every time a friend called, the friend saw Jews. And every time he went outside he both saw and heard Jews. It was unnerving. Nevertheless, he believed they would soon tire. But he was mistaken. They had a sacred cause and would not give in. Finally, on the sixth day, his will crumbled. He told their leaders that if they would go to the market place he would speak to them.

After the Jews had filed into the market, Pilate ordered it surrounded with soldiers—many of them vengeful Samaritans. Now with flashing armor to bolster his spirits, Pilate told the Jews cold-bloodedly that if they didn't quit pestering him about the images he would have them massacred.

Then Pilate had the surprise of his life. Here is how Josephus relates what happened: "But they threw themselves upon the ground, and laid their necks bare, and said they would take their death very willingly, rather than the wisdom of their laws should be transgressed."

Deeply moved, Pilate "commanded the images to be carried back from Jerusalem to Caesarea."

Thus, Caiaphas had his way!

The crowd that wouldn't enter the hall on the 15th day

Pontius Pilate

of Nisan pushed Jesus to the front and demanded action. By this time the face of Jesus was swollen by the blows He had received. His hair was matted and there was dry spittal on His cheeks.

"What accusation do you bring against this man?" asked Pilate lifting his jeweled hand for silence.

The answer came with the suddenness of a cattle whip. "If He were not a malefactor, we would not have delivered Him unto thee."

"Take Him and judge Him according to your own laws," said Pilate, squirming. He was determined to stay neutral and not get into another quarrel which might be reported to Rome.

"It is not lawful for us to put any man to death," replied a spokesman.

Getting to his feet, Pilate motioned for Jesus to enter with him into the ornate judgment hall. The two men were approximately the same age—both nearing the peak of their young manhood. After searching His face, Pilate asked: "Art thou the King of the Jews?"

"To this end was I born, and for this cause came I into the world, that I should bear witness unto the truth. Every one that is of the truth heareth My voice."

"What is truth?" demanded Pilate, a little startled. He then stepped out onto the game-scarred pavement, took his seat, and said to the mob, "I find no fault in him at all."

Pilate's words were met with a hiss of violent protest. The determined priests struck their foreheads with their fists and the Roman soldiers instinctively reached for their weapons. Then Pilate got an idea—an idea that would shift the responsibility to another. Somewhere in one of the conversations he had heard the word Galilee.

"This case is not for me," he said smoothly, chuckling inwardly at his cleverness, "it should be taken to Herod, Tetrarch of Galilee!"

But Herod Antipas—son of Herod the Great—didn't want to make a decision either. There was no value in sticking out one's neck, especially if it could be severed by Tiberius Caesar. And so after clothing Jesus in a purple robe and making sport of Him, he returned Him to Pilate.

This time Pilate was more direct. He knew Jesus had never uttered a word against the Roman government, or even against paying taxes. Moreover, he knew within the privacy of his heart that Jesus was without guilt. And so he pointedly said, "Ye have brought this man unto me, as one that perverteth the people; and, behold, I, having examined Him before you, have found no fault in this man touching those things whereof ye accuse Him."

At this, the crowd went wild. Their eyes and voices lashed at him like a typhoon-ridden sea. Desperately Pilate scrounged his mind for a way out. Then he remembered that it was customary to set a prisoner free on the day of the Feast of the Passover. He cleared his throat in order to make a suggestion. But even before he could speak a servant handed him a note from his wife.

The terse note said: "Have nothing to do with this just man: for I have suffered many things this day in a dream because of Him."

Pilate's eyes dilated and he could feel his heart thumping beneath his toga. He clenched his fists until his knuckles were white. Then, with a grim effort to keep his voice from trembling, he informed the mob that he would like to release a prisoner in order to follow the Passover custom. Next, he described Barabbas, a notorious criminal. "Whither of the twain will ye that I release unto you?" he asked.

"Away with the man," replied the crowd in one loud, unified voice, "and release unto us Barabbas."

But Pilate was still not ready to make a decision. Perhaps he could satisfy the Jews by having Jesus scourged. And so he gave the order for what was known as halfway death.

At a whipping post, Syrian soldiers tired themselves as they swung at Him with metal-tipped whips. And since this was Roman scourging they did not have to stop with thirty-nine stripes.

Finally, when Jesus was so weak He could barely stand, He was returned to Pilate. Facing the crowd, the ex-cavalry officer lifted Jesus' hand and cried, "*Ecce homo* [Behold the man]!" The crowd, however, wanted to see Him on a cross. Nothing else would satisfy them. All at once, like a Greek chorus, they began to chant, "Crucify Him! Crucify Him! Crucify Him!"

"Why, what evil hath He done?"

"Crucify Him! Crucify Him! Crucify Him!" was the terrifying answer.

Pilate still hesitated. He looked into the distorted faces of the frenzied mob, and he thought of Tiberius Caesar and his strict orders to keep peace in Judea. The jaws of the irresistible force and immovable object were rapidly and surely drawing together. An open grave seemed to gape before him.

Luke tells us that Pilate questioned the mob a third time. But again, he received the same deafening, unreasoning answer, "Crucify Him! Crucify Him! Crucify Him!"

His will completely shattered, Pilate called for a basin of water. Next, he slowly washed his hands and slowly dried them. Forcing the words from his parched lips, he slowly muttered, "I am innocent of the blood of this just person: see ye to it" (Matthew 27:24).

As Jesus was being led away to be crucified, Pilate opened the police blotter to the place where the record of judgments was kept. There, with a high sun winking on his jeweled hand, he wrote, "Jesus of Nazareth, scourged and crucified. April— A.U.C. 784." Although we know that this was April 7, according to our modern calendar, it would have been a different date in the days of Pilate owing to changes in the calendar—especially those made by Pope Gregory.

Having been involved in such high drama, many legends concerning Pilate have emerged. Josephus, however, has given us some stories that must be true.

Pontius Pilate

One of these concerns a Samaritan who inspired a crowd of Samaritans to climb Mount Gerizim with the promise that he would show them some sacred vessels which Moses had hidden there. Common sense should have told them, however, that Moses had never been there because of his death on Mount Nebo—many miles away—before the people of Israel ever crossed Jordan into the Promised Land.

"So they came thither armed," wrote Josephus, "and thought the discourse of the man probable; and as they abode at a certain village, which was called Tirathaba, they got the rest together to them, and desired to go up the mountain in a great multitude together; but Pilate prevented their going up by seizing upon the roads with a great band of horsemen and footmen, who fell upon those that were gotten together in the village; and when it came to an action, some of them they slew, and others of them they put to flight, and took a great many alive, the principal of which, and also the most potent of those that fled away, Pilate ordered slain."

Following this affair, Vitellius—Pilate's immediate superior—ordered him to Rome. But before Pilate arrived, Tiberius passed away on March 16, A.D. 37.

What followed is a mystery. Some say that Pilate was beheaded by Caligula; others, that he was beheaded by Nero. And still others claim that he committed suicide. A strong tradition declares that his head is buried on Mount Pilatus above Lake Lucerne in Switzerland. It is also suggested that Pilate's ghost, unable to find sanctuary, often returns to the lake and that one can hear it trying to wash the blood from its hands!

Another persistent legend says that Claudia became a convinced Christian. This legend has been so strong she was canonized by the Greek Orthodox Church.

66

CHAPTER 7

Claudius,
the Impossible

Perhaps because of the bloodthirstiness of Nero who followed him, and the eccentricities of Caligula who preceded him, Claudius has been neglected. This is a mistake, for Claudius—in his own impossible way—was as colorful as either of them. And since he ruled between A.D. 41 and 54—a time when Christian churches were being planted—his career is exceedingly important to students of the New Testament.

Born in Lyons in 10 B.C., Claudius was only a few years older than Jesus. But so strange was this mysterious man in his youth, his mother often described him as "a monster: a man whom Mother Nature had begun to work upon and then flung aside." And when she was upset with someone, she frequently exclaimed, "He's a bigger fool than even my son Claudius!"

The idea that Claudius was retarded was believed by the whole Imperial family. Deeply concerned, his great uncle, Augustus Caesar, wrote to the grandmother of Claudius about him. Said Augustus:

"My dear Livia,

"As you have suggested, I have now discussed with Tiberius what we should do about your grandson Claudius at the coming Festival of Mars the Avenger. We

Claudius

both agreed that an immediate decision ought to be taken. The question is whether he has—shall I say?—full command of his five senses. . . .

"I am against his watching the games in the Circus from the Imperial box, where the eyes of the whole audience would be upon him . . ." (Suetonius in *The Twelve Caesars*).

Augustus Caesar practically ignored him; and when Uncle Tiberius came to the throne, he treated him in the same manner. Thus neglected by relatives, Claudius began to associate with an unsavory class. He became addicted to gambling, and was frequently seen drunk.

How, then, did Claudius become the emperor? The answer to that is one of the most unique stories in history. But first we must have a glimpse of his genealogy.

The father of Claudius was Nero Claudius Drusus—a famous general and the first Roman to navigate the North Sea. Drusus died a year after Claudius was born. His mother was the young Antonia, daughter of the sister of Augustus—Octavia. Claudius was, therefore, the great-nephew of Augustus.

The royal blood of Claudius may have been even richer than what appears because of a curious event. His paternal grandmother, Livia Drusilla—mother of Drusus—was divorced from her first husband Tiberius Claudius Nero in 38 B.C. She then married Octavian—the future Augustus. However, Drusus was born a mere three months after this second marriage. And so even though legally Tiberius Claudius Nero was the father of Drusus, Octavian was suspected of being the real father. And he probably was!

These Imperial ties were further strengthened in A.D. 4 when Augustus adopted Tiberius—uncle of Claudius; and Tiberius, in turn, adopted Germanicus—brother of Claudius.

During the reigns of Augustus, Tiberius, and his nephew Caligula, Claudius was practically a nobody. When he wasn't drinking or gambling, he was reading

Claudius

and doing a little writing. He had a fondness for history. And then Caligula was assassinated. This changed everything!

When the assassins ordered the courtiers to disperse, Claudius hid behind a curtain. As he cringed in terror, a guard happened to notice his feet sticking out. The man jerked away the curtain, and then recognized Claudius. Thoroughly cowed, Claudius sank to the floor and grabbed the guard by the knees. He fully expected to be murdered on the spot.

But to his amazement, Claudius discovered from the astonished man that the Guard wanted him to be Emperor! At this time, the Senate was thoroughly disgusted with the antics of the insane Caligula. Many of them believed that Rome should once again become a Republic. The Guard, however, demanded a monarchy—and so did the crowds choking the streets. And since Claudius was a "simpleton" anyway, the shrugging Senate let the military have its way.

Claudius showed his appreciation to the Guard by presenting 15,000 sesterces to every member who had voted for him.

At the time of his election, Claudius was 50. Suetonius described him as being "tall, well-built, handsome, with a fine head of white hair and a firm neck, he stumbled as he walked owing to the weakness of his knees. . . ." (Will Durant suggests that at one time he had had polio.)

Often when he spoke, foam oozed from his mouth, and his nose ran. He suffered from gout, stuttered, and his head wobbled slightly as if it were attached to his shoulders by a spring. Also, he often fell asleep even when in public.

Having assumed the throne, he showed a generous spirit by offering amnesty to all who had agitated for a new constitution. Nevertheless he had the entire group of assassins who had murdered Caligula immediately put to death.

Claudius enjoyed sitting in judgment in court. Here, he

Claudius

liked to show what he considered to be his unusual wisdom. Once, when a woman along with a man appeared before him, there was a conflict as to whether or not the woman was the man's mother. Claudius solved the problem by requiring the woman to marry the man!

In another case in which the defendant was accused of posing as a Roman citizen, a dispute erupted as to whether the man should wear a Roman gown or a Greek mantle. Again Claudius solved the problem. His verdict was that he should wear the gown while he was being defended and the mantle when he was being accused.

Claudius was extremely susceptible to suggestion. Following the conviction of a man for forgery, the audience shouted, "He ought to have his hands cut off!" To this, Claudius responded immediately by asking that an executioner be brought with a block and cleaver.

The new emperor was devoted to his family line and liked to emphasize the greatness of his forebearers. His most frequent oath was "By Augustus!" He persuaded the Senate to vote divine honors for his grandmother Livia, and he insisted that her image as well as the image of Augustus be driven around the Circus in an elephant-drawn carriage during the ritual procession preceding the games.

A passion for gambling stayed with Claudius throughout his life. And so thoroughly addicted was he, he had a special board made for his carriage on which he could roll the dice without the dice falling off. Indeed, he loved throwing dice so much he wrote a book on the subject.

He was also attracted to gladiator shows; and when two combatants mortally wounded each other, he was so entranced he had their swords fashioned into pocketknives for his personal use. The flow of blood and human suffering excited him so much he decreed—says Suetonius—"that all combatants who fell accidentally should have their throats cut."

Whenever he could manage it, he liked to watch

Claudius

executions and the torture of prisoners. But so afraid was
he of his own death that he was constantly surrounded
with guards and "before entering a sickroom he always
had it carefully gone over: pillows and mattresses were
prodded, and bedclothes shaken out. Later, he even
required all visitors to be searched when they came to
pay him a morning call, and excused no one."

The marriages of Claudius were disasters. His first
wife died on their wedding day. The next two were
divorced. Then, at 48, he married Valeria Messalina who
was a mere 16. Messalina was far from beautiful. She had
a flat head, a deformed chest, and a florid face. Her
second child was a boy named Tiberius Claudius who
later came to be known as Britannicus in honor of the
conquest of Britain which took place in A.D. 43 under the
leadership of Claudius.

But Messalina was not satisfied in just being Queen of
the Roman Empire. Will Durant in *Caesar and Christ,*
tells us that "she fell in love with the dancer Mnester;
when he rejected her advances she begged her husband
to bid him to be more obedient to her requests; Claudius
complied, whereupon the dancer yielded to her
patriotically." Thus helped by her husband,
Messalina—spider-fashion—lured many into her bed.
Juvenal tells us that she even put on a disguise and
worked in a brothel.

Eventually, after she had committed bigamy by
marrying Caius Silius, Claudius ordered her death. He
then solemnly announced that he would never remarry,
and stated that if he did the Praetorian Guard was
authorized to kill him. And yet, within a year, he began to
plan for a new wife.

For a while Roman gossips were certain he would
marry Lollia, an ex-wife of Caligula. Lollia was
glamorous—and rich. She was frequently costumed in
jewels valued at 40,000,000 sesterces. Lollia, however,
could not compete with the wiles of Agrippina, daughter
of Germanicus, brother of Claudius, and the elder

Claudius

Agrippina. As a niece of Claudius, she could be more familiar with the Emperor than others.

Few women in history—including Jezebel—have been as cunning and deceitful as Agrippina. Agrippina had lived in incest with her brother Caligula, and had been widowed twice. She had broken up the home of her sister-in-law in order to marry her last husband, Caius Crispus. Caius was extremely wealthy, and after he had made out his will in her favor, he mysteriously died. Many think Agrippina poisoned him. Now, with her vast inheritance, she was one of the wealthiest women in the world.

Agrippina had four brazen goals. She was determined to marry Claudius, get rid of his son and heir Britannicus, persuade Claudius to adopt her red-headed son Nero, and to make Nero heir to the Empire.

Following a well-planned program of hugging and kissing Claudius whenever she could, Agrippina broke down his defenses. Since such a marriage was plainly incestuous, and since the Emperor had already referred to his bride-to-be as "my daughter and foster-child, born and bred in my lap so to speak" (Seutonius), he was embarrassed. Still, he followed a clever way out. He persuaded a group of senators to insist that the marriage was in the public interest!

At the time of the wedding, Claudius was 57 while Agrippina was only 32. Extremely jealous, the new bride had Lollia executed because Claudius, in an unguarded moment, had made flattering remarks about her figure. Soon Agrippina had so much power she insisted that she share the imperial dias with her husband. Next, she persuaded Claudius to adopt her son Nero.

During his reign, Claudius relied heavily on three freedmen—Narcissus, Pallas, and Callistus. These former slaves held the top posts in government. Moreover, all three, through the acceptance of bribes and the sale of office, became the richest men of antiquity.

Pallas, formerly owned by Antonia, the mother of Claudius, was a favorite in the palace. Students of the

New Testament are concerned with him, for he was a brother of Antonius Felix—procurator of Judea. It was before this former slave that Paul was tried (Acts 24:24,25).

Claudius was generally stern with corrupt officials. But he apparently never learned of the corruption and misrule of Felix because Pallas shielded him.

Josephus tells us that Felix was married three times, and that each wife was of royal blood. In addition, we are told that he had seduced each wife. At the time of the trial, he was married to Drusilla—daughter of Agrippa I and the former wife of the king of Emesa.

Felix, corrupt as he was, had a guilty conscience. Luke tells us, "And as he [Paul] reasoned of righteousness, temperance, and judgment to come, Felix trembled, and answered, Go thy way for this time; when I have a convenient season, I will call for thee" (Acts 24:25).

Luke also tells us about Felix's corruption, "He hoped also that money should have been given him of Paul, that he might loose him" (Acts 24:26). One wonders why Felix wanted a bribe from a poor man like Paul when his brother Pallas was estimated to be worth 300,000,000 sesterces.

The misrule of Felix in Judea can be seen by the fact that when the commander in Jerusalem decided to send Paul to Caesarea, 60 miles away, he had to take special precautions. Acts 23:14-24 tells the story. "See that you tell no man that you have revealed the plot to kill Paul," the commander told Paul's nephew as he sent him on his way. Paul's sister's son had sought out Paul to tell him that certain Jews were planning to kill him. Then the commander ordered a mount for Paul to ride and a bodyguard of 200 foot soldiers, 70 mounted horsemen, and 200 spearmen to assure the apostle's safe arrival to appear before Governor Felix!

That 470 men were required to deliver one prisoner to a city only a few miles away indicates that the Jews were rapidly arming themselves. Thus Felix was preparing for the outbreak of the Sicarii and the war that would break out with the Romans in A.D. 66.

That Christianity was being accepted among the Jews in Rome at this time is well known. But a note from Suetonius adds emphasis. "Because the Jews at Rome caused continuous disturbances at the instigation of Chrestus [Christ], he [Claudius] expelled them from the City."

Included with those who were expelled, was a couple, Aquila and Priscilla. Since these energetic Christians were tentmakers, they added Paul to their staff in Corinth, and they also were a great help to Apollos. Luke tells us, "They took him [Apollos] unto them, and expounded unto him the way of God more perfectly" (Acts 18:26). And thus, without knowing it, Claudius was a great help to Christianity.

Professor E.M. Blaiklock also thinks that Claudius may have made the first official reference to Christianity in a letter which he wrote in A.D. 41 to the people of Alexandria. Said Dr. Blaiklock: "There had recently been serious rioting between the Jewish and Gentile populations of the city, and Claudius addresses some sharp words of admonition to both parties. He tells the Jews that they must not invite illegal immigration into Alexandria of Jews from Syria or from other parts of Egypt, 'otherwise I will proceed against them with the utmost severity for fomenting a general plague which infests the whole world.' These final words so closely resemble language used elsewhere about Christianity (cf. Acts 24:5) that it has been suspected that the illegal immigrants from Syria might have been Christian missionaries" (The *Zondervan Pictorial Bible Atlas* edited by E.M. Blaiklock, 1969).

Claudius did not execute as many as did some of the other Roman emperors. But he accounted for his share. At least thirty-five senators and 300 knights lost their lives because of death warrants issued by him. Frequently forgetful, he sometimes ordered a man to be executed, forgot the order, and then wondered why the victim did not come to drink or roll dice with him.

In his spare time, this "stupid" man wrote books. His autobiography alone filled eight volumes; and his history of the Etruscans, written in Greek, filled another twenty. Thinking he could improve the Latin alphabet, he invented three new letters. One of these represented a vowel between *u* and *i*, and another took the place of the letters *ps*, and the third was a substitute for the consonantal form of *v*.

So prolific was Claudius, the library in Alexandria had a special wing to house his works.

How could such a simpleton do so much literary work? Claudius answered this by claiming that he had merely pretended to be a fool in order to escape execution at the hands of Caligula. This explanation, however, does not satisfy historians.

As Claudius aged, Agrippina exerted herself more and more. She sided with Pallas against Narcissus and had him condemned to a dungeon. She instituted a reign of terror and saw to it that the wealth of her victims was confiscated in order to bolster a depleted treasury. Deep in her heart was a fear that Claudius' son Britannicus would inherit the throne. She persuaded her husband to give his thirteen-year-old daughter Octavia to her sixteen-year-old Nero. Still she was afraid, for there was evidence that Claudius was beginning to see through her and that he was determined that Britannicus would be the new emperor.

Determined that this would never happen, Agrippina arranged for Claudius to be fed poisoned mushrooms. He died twelve hours later. He was in his sixty-fourth year.

Following a pompous funeral, the Senate voted him divine honors.

CHAPTER 8

They Call Him Nero

The shadows were lengthening across the warm hills of Rome as busy slaves erected final crosses in Nero's magnificent gardens. While they worked, soldiers brought in Christians and either tied them or nailed them to crosses. Next, they soaked them with inflammable pitch.

Darkness had frequently put a stop to the Emperor's chariot racing. This evening it would be different! The burning Christians would provide the light. Soon the chariots were lined up, the crosses were lit, and the horses leaped forward. As the clatter of the chariot wheels mingled, the crowds cheered. But there was no real enthusiasm in their cheers. Such flagrant cruelty was too much—even for them.

Seeing that he had displeased the crowd, Nero never repeated this performance. Instead, he contented himself by throwing Christians to the lions; by dressing them in animal skins and turning the dogs on them; and by killing those who were Roman citizens with the sword.

Today, Nero is remembered for his cruelties—and especially for having beheaded Paul. But strangely enough, in the beginning of his reign, he was immensely

Nero

popular because of his generosity, kindness, and even understanding. Shortly after becoming Emperor at the age of seventeen, he was asked to sign a criminal's death warrant. As he faced the document, he cried out in genuine anguish, "O, why was I ever taught to write?"

While Claudius was dying on October 13, A.D. 54, Agrippina made certain that his death was kept secret until all arrangements had been finalized to place Nero on the throne. Nero, of course, was ecstatic at his elevation—even though he knew the truth. After divine honors had been voted for his stepfather, he remarked, "Mushrooms must be the food of the gods, since by eating them Claudius has become divine!"

Being an atheist, Nero thought his little joke exceptionally funny.

Nero's first speech to the Senate aroused great enthusiasm. "He set forth," wrote Tacitus, "the principles and models by following which he hoped to administer the affairs of the Empire in the best manner. . . . In his house, he said, there should be no bribery nor corruption, nor anything to the wiles of ambition, and his family concerns should be kept distinct from the affairs of state. . . . "

The senators so loved his message, they had it engraved on a pillar of solid silver and decreed that it should be read publicly once a year.

Blue-eyed, freckle-faced Nero had reddish-bronze hair and slightly heavy cheeks. He was the son of Gnaeus Domitius—a member of the Ahenobarbi family. For five hundred years this family, noted for its red beards, blue blood, recklessness and courage, had been at the top of Roman society. Nero's paternal grandfather was extravagant and had a passion for gladiatorial shows. Likewise, he was cruel to his slaves. Indeed, he was so cruel he was denounced by Augustus.

Nero's father was a profligate noted for incest, brutality, and adultery. He married Nero's mother when she was a mere thirteen. Dio quotes him as having said,

Nero

"No good man can possibly come from us."

At his birth in A.D. 37 at Anzio, Nero was named Lucius Domitius Ahenobarbus. He retained this name until his mother married Claudius. When he was adopted by his stepfather his name was changed to Nero Claudius Drusus Germanicus.

The new emperor's boyish smile captivated almost everyone. But beneath that smile was an iron will. In the routine of things, he provided good government, grew slightly fat, raced his chariots, hired a voice teacher—and concentrated on singing.

Curiously, some of Nero's friends are well known to New Testament readers. His former tutor and current speech writer, Seneca, was the younger brother of Gallio who found Paul not "guilty of wrong or wicked lewdness," as recorded in Acts 18. And Vitellius, the senator who arranged with the Senate to legalize the marriage between his mother and Claudius, was a former governor of Syria. Indeed, it was he who dismissed Pontius Pilate. Also, Nero was the one who appointed Porcius Festus governor of Judea. Festus followed Felix and is one of the governors before whom Paul appeared (Acts 26:32).

Soon word filtered through to Nero that his mother was active in plots to take his life. At first he ignored these rumors and turned his attention onto Britannicus—his stepbrother and potent rival.

Finally, Nero decided that his stepbrother should die. Approaching his mother's old poison maker Locusta, he ordered a dose to be placed in Britannicus' drink. Alas, it merely acted as a laxative. He then summoned her, and after personally flogging her, sneered, "So you think I'm afraid of the Julian laws against poisoning?"

He then pulled her into his bedroom and stood over her while she made a concoction he deemed strong enough. But unwilling to take a chance, he first tried it out on a goat. And since it took the goat five hours to die, he had her boil it down to make it stronger. Next, he tried it on a pig, and when the pig died immediately, Nero was ready.

Nero

That February, a banquet was arranged for some of the highborn young people. Among those who attended were Britannicus and Titus—the youth who later destroyed Jerusalem. In the midst of the festivities on that warm, sticky night, a waiter brought Britannicus a cup of hot wine. After diluting it with cold water, Britannicus took the fatal sup.

As servants carried the unconscious lad out of the banquet hall, Nero assured the guests that he had merely had an epileptic seizure. By the following dawn, Nero had the body cremated at Campus Martius. Little was said of the sudden death of the former emperor's son. Nero's fame continued to soar.

Now he became convinced that his mother was against him, that the rumors he had heard were true. He also decided that his only way out was to kill her. But how was he to do this without exciting public opinion? After long consideration, he decided that she should die by accident! He arranged for her to go home on a ship that was due to capsize.

The boat sank as planned, but Agrippina swam to safety; and since it was night, those who were in on the plot, did not notice her escape. Nero then selected three officers to do the job.

When a startled Agrippina viewed their swords, she jerked her skirt open and screamed, "Strike at the womb that bore Nero!"

With both his mother and Britannicus dead, Nero behaved like a famished tiger suddenly released from its cage. While in conversation, a friend quoted a famous line: "When I am dead, may fire consume the earth."

Placing a hand on the man's shoulder, Nero corrected him at once by saying, "While *I am yet alive,* may fire consume the earth." And he proceeded to do this with alacrity. He poisoned the aunt who had raised him, tore up her will, and seized her estate. Then he banished Octavia, the sister of Britannicus whom he had married when he was sixteen. Twelve days later he married his mistress, Poppaea. Later, he ordered Octavia to commit suicide.

In honor of his new wife, he began the construction of the enormous Golden House—one of the wonders of the Empire. Set in vast gardens which included an artificial lake, he poured money into the new house with a lavish hand. Suetonius wrote: "Parts of the house were overlaid with gold and studded with precious stones. . . . All the dining rooms had ceilings of fretted ivory, the panels of which could slide back and let a rain of flowers, or of perfume from hidden sprinklers, shower upon his guests. The main dining-room was circular, and its roof revolved slowly, day and night, in time with the sky. Sea water, or sulpher water, was always on tap in the baths. When the palace had been decorated throughout in this lavish style, Nero dedicated it and condescended to remark: 'Good, now I can at last begin to live as a human being!' "

In this palace he indulged in all kinds of vice and made no effort to keep it secret. There was a huge bath where Poppaea bathed in mare's milk for her complexion. There was a vomitorium where guests could tickle their throats with a feather, lose their dinners, and stagger back to gorge some more. (Ruins of this can still be seen.) The walls were covered with the finest paintings and tapestries. And in the corners and other prominent places there were fountains and statues.

From boyhood, Nero had loved horses, and now chariot racing became a passion. Those who raced with him, however, knew that it was expedient to never win! Upon returning home from the races one evening, Poppaea chided him mildly for being late. Enraged by her remark, he booted her in the stomach, and since she was pregnant, she died. Brokenhearted, Nero ordered a state funeral and built a temple in her honor. And it is said that he burned Syria's entire annual crop of incense at her side. But the incense did not restore her life.

Too soon Nero forgot Poppaea for a new passion. "Having found a youth, Sporus, who closely resembled

Nero

The Golden House of Nero is a tourist attraction in modern Rome. Inset shows image of Nero which stands in front of the house.

Poppaea, he had him castrated, married him by a formal ceremony, and 'used him in every way like a woman'; whereupon a wit expressed the wish that Nero's father had had such a wife" (Will Durant in *Caesar and Christ*).

Nero's interest in the arts continued. He had a slender talent. He began to write poetry, to paint—and especially to sing. Soon he fancied that he was one of the world's truly great singers. He entered into singing contests all over the Empire. The prizes were always his—and he gloated over them. In Athens, the audience gave him such an ovation he declared that from then on Greece was to have dominion status. And at this the audience cheered even more!

Nero had been reigning about ten years when suddenly on July 19, A.D. 64, a fire broke out in Rome. The blaze started in some wooden sheds just east of the Circus Maximus. Soon it spread to the foot of the Palatine and Caelian Hills where vast quantities of oil and other inflammables had been stored. In those days the streets of Rome were very narrow and the flames leaped from one house to the next.

The fire raged on for six days and as the buildings fell thieves got busy looting, murdering, destroying.

When it seemed the conflagration had burned itself out, it started again and burned for another three days. By the time the fire was out, more than two-thirds of Rome was in ashes. Nero was terribly shaken—especially because the libraries and museums had been destroyed. He worked hard to take care of the refugees. He erected a city of tents for them in the Field of Mars, and brought in supplies of food for which he paid out of his own pocket.

And then one sultry night he was seen on the tower of a garden theater across the Tiber where he had established his headquarters. There was a lyre in his hands, and while the crowd watched in horrified silence, he began to sing about the sack of Troy while he accompanied himself on the lyre. Soon word spread that Nero had set

Nero

the fire. Such accusations were even scrawled on public buildings. Nero became desperate for a scapegoat to blame. Soon he found one.

In the words of Tacitus, he directed his fury against "a race of men detested for their evil practices, and commonly called Chrestiani. The name was derived from Chrestus, who, in the reign of Tiberius, suffered under Pontius Pilate, Procurator of Judea. By that event the sect of which he was founder received a blow which for a time checked the growth of the dangerous superstition; but it revived soon after, and spread with recruited vigor not only in Judea . . . but even in the city of Rome, the common sink into which everything infamous and abominable flows like a torrent from all quarters of the world" (Annals 15:44).

With infinite cunning, Nero incited the Romans against the Christians. Tacitus wrote: "They were put to death with exquisite cruelty, and to their sufferings Nero added mockery and derision.... At length the brutality of these measures filled every breast with pity. Humanity relented in favor of the Christians."

After the debris had been cleared, Nero started to rebuild. Funds were called in from throughout the Empire and they were used to rebuild the homes of the citizens, with no cost to them. Streets were widened and straightened. Water reservoirs were arranged so that another general fire could not take place—and the city was beautified. Indeed, such a fine job was done, enthusiasts wanted to change the name of the city from Rome to Nero!

Nero's fame leaped higher every day. The Senate even suggested starting the new year with December, the month of his birth, rather than the customary January. When he refused the honor, his popularity leaped even higher. Exaggerated stories were told about his kindness. It was said that when he learned of the illness of a friend, he sent all the way to Egypt for a doctor to treat him. It was also claimed that he wanted to eliminate indirect taxes throughout the Empire.

Soon Nero was confronted with a different type of trouble. During the winter of 65 and the spring of 66, plague broke out in Rome. Within weeks thirty thousand were dead and neither graves nor funeral pyres could be prepared fast enough. Many blamed Nero, saying that he had offended the gods.

Nero became extremely sensitive to criticism. Once "a comedian named Datus, who had to say the lines 'Goodbye, Father; goodbye, Mother!' in a play in which he was acting, pretended to be eating something which disagreed with him . . . (and he) made the motions of a swimmer, his reference being, of course, to the poisoned mushrooms given to Claudius and to the shipwreck of Agrippina. Nero banished him from the capital for his audacity" (*Nero* by Arthur Weigall. Garden City Publishing Co, 1930.)

From this point, his popularity plunged. The army revolted in Spain and Galba was declared the new emperor. The Senate now decreed that Nero was an outlaw. He fled from Rome in disguise. Cornered on a June evening, he crept into a basement, and there, shivering on a dirty cot, he tried to commit suicide. But the knife did not penetrate his throat deep enough; and so he begged his servant, Epaphroditus, to press the blade home. As he died, it is reported that he murmured, "What a great artist dies with me!" He was thirty-one and had ruled fourteen years.

By a remarkable coincidence, he died on June 9th, the anniversary of the date when he forced Octavia to commit suicide.

As we look at the grisly reign of Nero, we cannot help but remember that in the days of his greatest popularity Paul shivered in the Mamertine prison near the Forum. From this place it is quite possible that he could hear the cheers of the senators as they clapped and shouted their approval of Nero. But things have a way of reversing themselves. In our time the words of this curly-haired

Nero

emperor are either forgotten or despised, while the epistles of Paul—many written in this very prison—are loved and quoted everywhere.

Today there is a common saying about these two contemporaries. That saying is this: "We name our sons Paul; but we name our dogs Nero!"

CHAPTER 9

Titus —He Crushed Jerusalem

Caligula's brazen announcement that he would have his statue erected in the Holy of Holies in Jerusalem filled the Jews with unspeakable horror. Nothing had stirred them so much since Antiochus Epiphanes had sacrificed a pig on the altar of the Temple. This was because erecting a statue was a direct violation of the commandment, "Thou shalt not make unto thee any graven image."

The Jews hoped that Caligula was merely teasing, for it was known throughout the Empire that he had a twisted sense of humor. But Little Boot was not teasing. He dispatched Petronius to Judea with an army along with orders to set up the statue even if it meant war.

Petronius invaded the country with two legions of Roman soldiers. Still, the Jews would not give in. They approached him by the tens of thousands and told him plainly that they would rather die than to have the statue erected. The bitter argument churned for months. Finally Petronius agreed that he would write to Rome and see if he could get the order changed. The moment he had finished speaking, a heavy, unexpected rain began to fall. And since it had not rained for a year, the Jews were confident that God was showing His approval to

Titus

their resistance by ending the draught.

In Rome, Caligula's old friend, Herod Agrippa I, prepared a lavish dinner for the Emperor. Caligula was so pleased he told Agrippa that he should ask for a gift—any gift—and that he would bestow it. Agrippa then asked that his statue not be erected in the Temple. And although Little Boot was mildly shocked by the request, he agreed at once.

Having thus defied Rome and gotten away with it, the Jews—especially the Zealots—gripped their daggers in an even firmer grip and proceeded to defy their rulers in other matters. Unrest in the land continued to grow, and the blundering maleficence of Antonius Felix tended to bring this unrest to a climax. The breaking point came in May, A.D. 66 when the procurator, Florus, took seventeen talents from the Temple.

Some of the young people responded to this by carrying around baskets to gather money for the "poverty-stricken" ruler. This sarcasm infuriated Florus. He summoned his legions, looted hundreds of homes, and killed thousands. Many leading Jews were scourged and spiked to crosses. This slaughter ended in all out war.

Joseph—now known as Josephus—was made the Jewish commander for all of Galilee. Nero responded by sending General Titus Flavius Vespasianus to lead the Roman legions. Square-jawed and nearly bald, Vespasian had distinguished himself in the conquest of Britain and thus seemed an ideal choice. Along with his son Titus he swooped down on Galilee from the north; and there, in the area where Jesus had preached, he won a stunning victory. He made six thousand slaves and sent them to Corinth to dig Nero's famous canal. Among the captives was Josephus.

By October, A.D. 67, all of Galilee had been subdued. In the summer of the next year, long before the rebellion was crushed, Nero committed suicide.

Nero's death was followed by chaos. While the war was still raging in Judea, a message telling of Nero's death was sent to Servius Sulpicius Galba in Spain 332 miles away and it reached him in a record time of thirty-six hours. Upon arriving in Rome in June of 68, this former governor-general of Greater Germany, donned the purple.

Galba was addicted to most of the vices that afflicted his predecessors—including a passion for execution. Suetonius says: "He sentenced men of all ranks to death without trial on the scantiest of evidence, and seldom granted applications for Roman citizenship." Still, he ruled with some justice, and he had a passion for economy. He was far from well and could not wear shoes due to his misshapen feet, twisted and swollen by gout.

The leading politicians were unhappy because they could not freely dip into the treasury, thus his popularity soon ended. While marching to the Forum, the Guard intercepted him as he was being carried on a litter. Told that he must die, he thrust out his neck and his head was hacked off. Next, they sheared away his lips and chopped off his arms. A soldier then attempted to pick up the head by the hair. But since the hair was too slippery from blood, he stuck his thumb into the mouth and carried the trophy to Otho as a symbol of his call to mount the throne.

Otho presented the blue-eyed trophy to a group of servants. These men placed it on the end of a spear and paraded with it around the camp chanting:

> Galba, Galba, Cupid Galba,
> Please enjoy your vigor still.

Galba's reign lasted only six months.

Marcus Salvius Otho had been a senator. Bankrupt, he declared, "I might as well fall to some enemy as to my creditors in the Forum." He suggested that the only way he could square his accounts was by being made Emperor.

A sympathetic Senate—made even more sympathetic by bribery and conspiracy—complied. In the meantime the army in Germany hailed Quintus Vitellius—son of the governor of Syria who had dismissed Pontius

Titus

Pilate—Emperor. Vitellius had been a favorite at court, and had a certain earthy wisdom. After Caligula had declared that the moon-goddess had descended to embrace him, he inquired if Vitellius could see her. "No," the latter replied, "only you gods can see one another."

After several battles with Vitellius upon his invasion of Italy, Otho decided that his chance of survival was hopeless. Following a night with two daggers under his pillow, Otho plunged one of them into his side at dawn. At the time of his death he was thirty-five. His reign had lasted only ninety-five days.

At the news of Otho's death, Vitellius marched on Rome in full uniform and took the throne. Nero was his model and he started his reign by making a sacrifice to him. Vitellius was an accomplished glutton. He often gorged at three or four feasts in a single day. His taste was exotic and he craved such things as peacock brains, flamingo tongues, and pike livers.

Thoroughly disgusted with the performance of this man, Vespasian, while still battling in Judea, sent Antonius, one of his generals, to Italy in order to dethrone the "imposter." After one of the bloodiest battles in history, Antonius prevailed and entered Rome. Vitellius was dragged from his hiding place, and with a noose around his neck was pulled half naked through the streets of the city amidst the taunts of the crowd who called him such names as "greedy-guts." After he had been killed, his corpse was attached to a hook and dragged through a few more streets and then flung into the Tiber.

At the time of his death, Vitellius was fifty-six. There are conflicting reports as to the length of his reign. However, all are agreed that it was less than one year.

Before Vespasian hurried away to Rome to don the purple, he placed his son Titus in charge of the Jewish war.

The moon was riding high when Titus appeared before Jerusalem with 80,000 men. There were regular troops,

90

engineers, and cavalry—and sprinkled among these veterans were many Arabs. At the time of his appearance, the Holy City was overflowing with devout pilgrims who had come to celebrate Passover.

As Titus appeared, a fierce civil war was going on behind the walls. Zealots and moderates were stabbing each other and the streets were turning crimson. When Titus demanded surrender, the Jews laughed with scorn and continued to hack at one another.

The Romans now drew siege engines to the northern wall and began operations. These engines—scorpiones and ballistae—were capable of tossing one hundred pound stones six hundred feet. As the stones thudded the walls, the factions within the city united to fight a common invader. Soon a large hole was smashed in the northern wall. Five days later the second wall was pierced and the dusty legions streamed through. Here a bloody hand-to-hand battle seesawed back and forth. Ultimately the northern section was in Roman hands.

Titus now decided on new strategy—psychological warfare. He determined to frighten the city into submission. Accordingly, he issued orders for the men to don their smartest regalia, polish their shields and armor, and costume their horses with their brightest displays. Then he ordered them to solemnly march past while he doled out pay and rations. And so for four days the legions tramped by in full view of the Jews on the walls and behind spy holes.

But the Jews were not impressed!

Still thinking there must be an easy way to get Jerusalem to surrender, Titus sent Josephus—his former enemy—to plead with the people. He felt that the defeated commander of Galilee would have a special influence on his kinsmen. Josephus found a place on the wall where he was relatively safe from arrows, and began to beg the people to surrender. His long speech concluded with this paragraph: "O miserable creatures! are you so unmindful of those who used to assist you, that

Titus

you will fight by your weapons and by your hands against the Romans? When did we ever conquer any other nation by such means? and when was it that God, who is the creator of the Jewish people, did not avenge them when they had been injured?"

But the defenders were not ready to surrender. Titus then had ramps built and placed siege engines on top so that he could hurl boulders even further into the city. Failing with this method, he resolved to starve them out. A wall—circumvallatio—was built around the city. This nearly stopped the brave ones who had been slipping in and out in the darkness in order to get supplies.

Nevertheless, there were still desperate men who would do anything to escape the besieged city that was already filled with the stench of the dead and dying. Such men swallowed jewels and bits of gold, thus hoping to smuggle their treasure out. Few escaped. Greedy Roman soldiers hunted them down, ripped them open, and groped through their entrails for the valuables. Also, Titus ordered that anyone caught outside the city was to be crucified. Altogether, says Josephus, about five hundred were crucified every day. To find wood for the crosses and ramps, every tree in the area was cut down. Even the Mount of Olives was laid bare.

Still the Jews would not surrender!

Famine now came to the city with a vengeance. Death was everywhere. Josephus who was on the outside and whose family was on the inside recorded the events carefully. "Then did the famine widen its progress, and devoured people by whole houses, and families. ... As for burying them, those that were sick themselves were not able to do it ... the lanes of the city were filled with dead bodies. ... A deep silence also, and a kind of deadly night, had seized the city; while yet the robbers were still more terrible than the miseries themselves; for they brake open the houses which were no other than the graves of the dead bodies, and plundered them of what they had. ... Now everyone of these died with their eyes fixed on the

Temple."

Cannibalism of the most flagrant kind was practiced. Josephus records that even Titus was appalled. "However, when Titus, in going his rounds along these valleys, saw them full of dead bodies, and the thick putrefaction running about them, he gave a groan; and spread out his hands to heaven and called God to witness that this was not his doing."

Even as the people starved, battering rams were crashing into the walls. Finally, at the beginning of July, the Tower of Antonia—named in honor of Mark Antony—fell to the Romans. This tower stood close to the Temple. The soldiers were now anxious to capture this magnificent place of worship known throughout the Roman Empire as one of the wonders of the world. Some of the officers thought it would make an ideal fortress. But Titus opposed them. He did not want the Temple damaged.

However, in the heat of the battle, some of the legionnaires lost their heads. A soldier tossed a flaming torch through the Golden Window into the Holy of Holies. Filled with jars of holy oil and old paneling, the sacred room was soon an oven of flames.

Horrified, Titus ordered the fire quenched. But the men were not interested in putting it out, and perhaps even if they had been it would have been an impossibility.

Crazed by success, Titus went to unbelievable extremes. "Caesar ordered the whole city and the Temple to be razed to the ground. He left standing only the towers of Phasael, Hippicus, Mariamne, and a part of the wall on the west side." Josephus adds that 97,000 prisoners were taken and that 115,800 corpses were removed from the city. In that terrible month of August, A.D. 70, the Temple was destroyed and it has never been rebuilt, although Julian the Apostate made such an attempt during his short reign—A.D. 360-363.

Jerusalem with its 600,000 inhabitants had been humiliated.

Titus

The Arch of Titus in Rome honors the destruction of Jerusalem by Titus in A.D. 70. Inside the arch, relief pictures show Temple treasures being carried off.

Titus

Titus returned to Rome with his Jewish mistress, Bernice—sister of the King Agrippa before whom Paul made his appeal (Acts 25:23). With thousands of Jewish slaves in chains behind him, and with the spoils of victory in the hands of his men, he marched in triumph through the city on the Tiber.

An arch celebrating this triumph was then erected near the Forum, and even to this day it stands in excellent condition. Titus wanted to marry Bernice, but he was dissuaded by Vespasian. After the death of Vespasian's wife, he had lived in common law with a freedwoman, and following her death, with a number of concubines. And the Emperor felt that his son could do the same.

In A.D. 72, Vespasian started to build the huge Flavian Amphitheater—commonly known today as the Colosseum. The building which was designed to seat from 60-80,000 was 620 feet long and 513 feet wide. It was named in honor of the obscure Flavian family from which Vespasian was descended.

Seven years after the building had been started, Vespasian suddenly felt a spell of giddiness. "Alas, I think I am becoming a god," he said with his wry sense of humor. Then he struggled to his feet while he muttered, "An emperor should die standing." With these last words he passed away and Titus became the new emperor.

At the time of Vespasian's death, he was nearly seventy.

With the help of thousands of Jewish slaves, Titus finished the Flavian Amphitheater where so many thousands of Christians were to be martyred. The dedication took place in A.D. 80, and Titus decreed that the dedicatorial celebrations should last 100 days.

During the period of dedication, five thousand animals lost their lives. Lions were pitted against elephants, bears against bulls, and, alas, men against men.

Nothing seemed to please the people more than a cataract of blood. Perhaps Titus was inspired by the

Titus

The Roman Colosseum was completed by Titus after his destruction of Jerusalem (above). Below, inside view shows the dungeons and lion enclosures that were below the flooring.

butchery in Jerusalem during his most glorious days. He passed away in his forty-second year while visiting the same house in which his father had died. His rule had lasted only a little more than two years and two months. Pious Jews said that he suffered an early death because he had desecrated the Holy of Holies.

What happened to the Jerusalem Christians during this terrible time? Eusebius, the first church historian (A.D. 260?-340), says: "Furthermore, the members of the Jerusalem church, by means of an oracle given by revelation to acceptable persons there, were ordered to leave the City before the war began and settled down in a town in Peraea called Pella" (*The History of the Church* by Eusebius, Penquin Classics).

If John Mark, as many scholars believe, wrote the Gospel that bears his name in this period, it is significant that one will find no bitterness in his book concerning the destruction of Jerusalem. This lack of bitterness is all the more remarkable when we remember that strong tradition says that Mark's mother owned considerable property within the city. The solution is that John Mark had found the *Other City* and was quite satisfied.

The loss of property is not catastrophic to those who know Christ!

CHAPTER 10

Domitian —He Exiled John

Among the many Roman emperors whose fingers were smudged with the blood of Christians was Domitian, son of Vespasian, and younger brother of Titus. He was the last of the Flavians.

Second only to Nero in cruelty in this period, Domitian's proscriptions included members of his own family. Included within his bloodthirsty goals was a determination to execute all descendants of King David's line. And numbered with these were the grandsons of Jude—brother of Jesus.

Unfortunately we do not have the names of many of Domitian's victims. But this sinister fact adds even more grimness to the horror of his tyranny. The names were not recorded for the obvious reason that Christians were considered far too insignificant to have their names written down. To Domitian, murdering a Christian was like swatting a fly.

One of his would-be victims, however, is known. Early Christian writers assure us that it was Domitian who persecuted John the Revelator. At first he had him arrested in Ephesus where he was doing a mighty work in the church. Then he brought him to Rome and had him tossed into a cauldron of boiling oil that seethed and

Domitian

bubbled in front of the Latin Gate.

Having escaped death from the oil by a miracle, John was banished as a slave to the stone quarries on the Isle of Patmos. It was there he had his colorful visions and wrote the book which is associated with his name.

As was generally the case, the problem that wedged itself between Domitian and the Christians was that of the Emperor's self-deification. The Christians, as Paul had admonished in Romans thirteen, tried to obey him as their ruler, but they absolutely refused to worship him—even though that worship entailed the mere burning of a few grains of incense. And this was an extremely sore point, for Domitian stubbornly insisted that he was divine. After he took back his divorced wife Domitia, he referred to his action as "a recall to my divine bed." Also, he encouraged the masses to cheer him and his wife in the Colosseum with the shout, "Long live our Lord and Lady!"

In a brazen letter to the Senate, Domitian began with the words: "Our Lord God instructs you to do this." Indeed, he insisted that he was not just a god, but God! He even went so far as to rule that whenever he was referred to in documents, he was to be mentioned as *Dominus et Deus Noster*—Our Lord and God."

Such stark blasphemy was too much for the Christians—and the Jews. Yes, even the Romans shuddered!

From the time of Domitian's birth on October 24, A.D. 51 in Rome's Pomegranate Street, conflicts began to writhe and lash within his mind. His brother Titus was ten years older and as the heir-apparent received most of the attention. During official parades, Titus rode up front with Vespasian seated in a coveted curule chair while Domitian tagged behind in a litter.

This rivalry between himself and his brother increased with the years. And it was given a decided boost when Titus returned to Rome for a hero's welcome after destroying Jerusalem. In the gala parade that swept

Domitian

through the important avenues, Titus and his father were given most of the credit.

When Titus ascended the throne at the time of Vespasian's death, Domitian declared that his father's will had been altered and that he should have shared the Empire. Titus offered to share power with him, but Domitian angrily refused the offer. Instead, he began to plot both privately and openly. One of his plots, unashamedly designed to gather public approval, was "offering his troops twice as large a bounty as Titus had offered them." He also planned military conquests in which he could shine.

But events changed sooner than Domitian had dared to hope. Titus fell seriously ill. Domitian rushed to his bedside, and one way or another quickened his death. One source has it that he covered him with snow. Suetonius claimed that he "told the attendants to presume his death by leaving the sick-bed before he had actually breathed his last."

In this manner, Domitian ascended the throne.

Domitian is remembered as a vain and lazy man. He had a ruddy complexion, was tall and strong, had large moon-like eyes, and was exceedingly proud of his hair. As a matter of fact, he was so proud of his hair, he wrote a book entitled *Care of the Hair*. But as often happens, he soon lost his hair, developed a paunch, and his once solid legs became thin and spindly with hammer-like toes.

Upon assuming power, Domitian tried to get the Empire to forget Titus as soon as possible. Whenever he was forced to refer to him, he did so indirectly. Nevertheless, probably because of public opinion, Domitian was compelled to complete the Arch of Titus raised in memory of his brother's victory over the Jews.

Having become Emperor, Domitian seemed bored with his work. In the early days, it is said that he spent much of his time catching flies. He liked to spear them with a pen. When an important visitor asked if someone was with the Emperor, Vivius Crispus is alleged to have

Domitian

replied: "No, not even a fly." This story became one of the behind-the-hand jokes of the time.

Like Nero and others, Domitian tried to rule with moderation and justice—in the beginning. During those first years he attempted to stamp out immorality. An unchaste Vestal Virgin was executed. He outlawed the making of eunuchs and lowered their price on the slave market in order to discourage the practice. He stopped the ritual sacrifice of oxen and outlawed indecent pantomime. He even refused legacies if it could be shown that they would impoverish the children.

Thinking the Empire needed the steadying influence of religion, Domitian set out to encourage the old Roman faiths. During the great fires of 79 and 82, the Temple of Jupiter, Juno, and Minerva had been destroyed. He ordered this Temple rebuilt and lavished it with gold plated doors and a gilded roof. The new building cost over 50,000,000 sesterces—an amount that caused the Senate to wince.

Domitian encouraged sculpture, poetry, and music. He even wrote poetry himself. He rebuilt libraries and searched the Empire for the finest volumes. Indeed, he ruled with creative ability for several years. Then, like Nero and Caligula, he became drunk with power. A cruel and haughty spirit completely possessed him. He altered his name to Germanicus and then renamed the months of September and October to Germanicus and Domitianus. The reason? He was born in October and became Emperor in September!

He decreed that images of himself be placed throughout the city and that those in more prominent places be made of silver or gold. He even stipulated the minimum weight of the precious metal.

With uncontrolled arrogance, Domitian became so suspicious of others he ordered executions at the slightest cause. Offended by some allusions in an historical work of Hermogenes of Tarsus, he ordered him put to death and had the slaves who had copied the work crucified.

Domitian

One person was killed because he insisted on celebrating the birthday of his uncle, the former emperor Otho. Another was put to death merely because he resembled a man Domitian hated.

Executing people became a sport, as did all kinds of torture. One of the tortures Domitian developed was that of scorching a victim's genitals. Once he invited a man to dine with him even though he had secretly ordered his crucifixion on the following day. All of this, of course, made Domitian fear for his own life. This fear soon became such an obsession he had the place where he took his daily walk lined with mirrors. Thus he was able to glance in several directions and avoid assassination.

Since both Domitian's father and brother had been in Jerusalem, he had undoubtedly heard of the Jewish belief in the coming of the Messiah, and he had also heard of the second coming of Jesus Christ. These beliefs frightened him, and like Herod the Great, he decided to do something about it. Many Christians who refused to burn incense to Domitian were liquidated. Among these was his own nephew Flavius Clemens.

Through Jewish prophecy, he learned that the Messiah was to be from the descendants of David. He therefore decided that he would eliminate all these descendants. Because of this determination, he arrested the grandsons of Jude. As he faced them, he demanded to know how much money they possessed. The men replied that they had a mere twenty-five acres between them. Holding up calloused hands, they explained how difficult it was to scratch a living from their unproductive soil. Impressed with their seeming honesty, Domitian began to inquire about Jesus and His kingdom.

"When asked about Christ and his kingdom—what it was like, and where it would appear—they explained that it was not of this world or anywhere on earth but angelic and in heaven, and would be established at the end of the world, when he would come in glory to judge

Domitian

the quick and the dead. . . . On hearing this, Domitian found no fault with them, but despising them as beneath his notice let them go free and issued orders terminating the persecution of the Church. On their release they became leaders of the churches, both because they had borne testimony and because they were of the Lord's family; and thanks to the establishment of peace they lived on into Trajan's time" (*The History of the Church* by Eusebius).

Thus, through a miracle, thousands were spared.

But although Domitian stopped persecuting Christians, he continued his tyranny. In 96 he suddenly became suspicious of his secretary Epaphroditus. Casting about for an excuse to execute him, he remembered that Epaphroditus had helped Nero commit suicide twenty-seven years before. (This Epaphroditus is alleged to have been a convert to Judaism; thus he was not the man who took the gift to Paul from the Philippian Church.) Because of this, he had him killed. This so frightened the other workers in Domitian's household, they decided to assassinate him. Domitian's wife, Domitia, joined the conspiracy.

At the agreed time, the servants burst into the royal bedroom and after a brief skirmish the man who had ruled for fiteen years was dead. When the Senate learned of his death, they ordered all his statues destroyed and all the inscriptions mentioning him defaced.

And thus it was that the man who considered himself to be God, and who demanded that the world worship him, was killed by his own wife and a few servants. At the time of his death, September 18, A.D. 96, he had ruled fourteen years. He was only forty-four.

Domitian was denied a public funeral.

CHAPTER 11

That Famous Trajan Letter

Following the death of Domitian, Nerva—considered one of "the five good emperors"—ascended the throne at the age of sixty-six. Nerva recalled many of Domitian's exiles, lowered taxes, and put a stop to executions.

But the Praetorian Guard did not like him. His economies cramped their style, and so they stormed the palace. Without resisting, Nerva offered them his throat. Miraculously, however, they spared him on condition that he adopt a son to follow him who would be acceptable to both the Senate and the Guard.

Nerva adopted Marcus Ulpius Trainus—known today as Trajan. And after a rule of only sixteen months, Nerva was replaced by Trajan. Trajan was heading a Roman army in Cologne at the time of his election. But instead of rushing to Rome to enjoy the honor, he remained at his post for nearly two years in order to complete some projects he had started. This was characteristic.

This tall, handsome man is remembered today for many things. He was a great builder, an able and hard working administrator, had the courage of a lion, and was generally a man of simple tastes. In addition, his troops loved him. But oddly enough, Christendom's memories of Trajan do not center around these things.

Trajan

Instead, he is remembered best for a letter—a letter which he probably dashed off in a few minutes without too much thought.

The reason this letter is so famous is because it is the first official letter from a Roman Emperor which specifically names and concerns itself with Christians. (In the letter of Claudius mentioned previously, it is merely *assumed* that he was referring to Christians. Also, they are not identified.) This letter—found in Paris in 1500—is in regard to the martyrdom of Christians. And among those who died as a result of this correspondence was the revered Polycarp, Bishop of Smyrna.

Pliny—nephew and adopted son of Pliny the Elder—had been sent to Bithynia as *corrector civitatium* and was answerable to Trajan. By this time Christianity was becoming known as something more than just a sect in Judaism. Also, it was spreading rapidly. In Asia Minor there were churches at Ephesus, Colossae, Laodicea, Hierapolis, Sardis, Pergamum, Smyrna, Philadelphia—and other places. This new faith presented a problem he did not understand. And being a lawyer by profession, Pliny was anxious to do everything in a legal way.

A basic tenet of Roman rule was not to interfere with the religious beliefs of its subjects. Thus the Jews were not forced to eat pork and they were allowed to practice circumcision. There were, of course, emperors who violated this law.

There was a time when the emperors could merely shrug at Christianity. But that time had ended. Upon taking his position in Bithynia, Pliny learned that Christianity was a force in that area. Peter's first epistle was addressed to the Jewish Christians "scattered throughout Pontus . . . and Bithynia" (I Peter 1:1). Also Luke, the New Testament's prolific author, had died—probably by hanging—in Bithynia. Puzzled about what he should do, Pliny sought the advice of Trajan.

After greetings and assurances of loyalty, he wrote:

"I am unacquainted as to the method and limits to be observed in examining and punishing them. Whether, therefore, any difference is to be made with respect to age ... between the young and the adult; whether repentance admits to pardon; or if a man has once been a Christian, it avails him nothing to recant; whether the mere profession of Christianity, albeit without any criminal act, or only the crimes associated therewith are punishable; in all these points I am greatly doubtful.

"In the meantime the method I have observed toward those who have been denounced to me as Christians, is this: I interrogated them whether they were Christians; if they confessed I repeated the question twice again, adding a threat of capital punishment; if they still persevered, I ordered them to be executed; for I was persuaded, that whatever the nature of their creed, a contumacious and inflexible obstinacy certainly deserved chastisement. There were others also brought before me possessed with the same infatuation: but being citizens of Rome, I directed them to be carried thither.

"These accusations, from the mere fact that the matter was being investigated, began to spread, and several forms of mischief came to light. A placard was posted up without any signature, accusing a number of people by name. Those who denied that they were Christians, or had ever been so, who repeated after me an invocation to the gods, and offered religious rites with wine and frankincense to your statue (which I had ordered to be brought for the purpose, together with those of the gods), and finally cursed the name of Christ (none of which, it is said, those who are really Christians can be forced into performing), I thought proper to discharge. Others who were named by the informer at first confessed themselves Christians, and then denied it; true, they had been of that persuasion formerly, but had now quitted it (some three years, others many years, and a few as much as twenty-five years ago). They all worshipped your

Trajan

statue and the images of the gods, and cursed the name of Christ.

"They affirmed, however, that the whole of their guilt or their error was, that they met on a certain fixed day before it was light and sang an antiphonal chant to Christ, as to a god, binding themselves by a solemn oath, not to any wicked deeds, but to never commit any fraud, theft or adultery, never to falsify their word, nor deny a trust when they should be called upon to deliver it up; after which it was their custom to separate, and then reassemble to partake of food—food of an ordinary innocent kind. . . .

"I therefore thought it proper to adjourn all further proceedings in this affair, in order to consult with you. For the matter is well worth referring to you, especially considering the numbers endangered: persons of all ranks and ages, and of both sexes, are and will be involved in the prosecution. For this contagious superstition is not confined to the cities only, but has spread through the villages and countryside. Nevertheless it seems still possible to check and cure it. . . ." (*Private Letters, Pagan and Christian,* compiled by Dorothy Brooke, E.P. Dutton & Co., 1930).

Trajan replied:

"The method you have pursued, my dear Pliny, in sifting the cases of those denounced to you as Christians is eminently proper. . . . *No search should be made for these people* [italics mine]; when they are denounced and found guilty they should be punished; but when the accused party denies that he is a Christian, and gives proof . . . by adoring our gods, he shall be pardoned. . . . Information without the accuser's name subscribed shall not be admitted in evidence against anyone" (*Pliny the Younger, Letters,* Loeb Library).

This policy of not prosecuting Christians unless they were accused was generally followed during Trajan's reign. But although he did not instigate wholesale persecutions as did Nero, he did execute many. Among his victims, were Ignatius, Bishop of Antioch; and Cleophas, a reputed cousin of Jesus Christ.

Trajan soon tired of administrative work. War was the passion of his life. Following two long Dacian campaigns, he turned his legions to the East. He overran Armenia and northern Mesopotamia and added these countries to his Empire. Then, exulted by success, he continued on down the Tigris River to the Persian Gulf. Stooped by age and fatigue, he longed for the youth of Alexander the Great.

Soon enemies on both sides began to attack. He lost much of what he had conquered. But with a mighty effort he gained some of it back. Then, while in the midst of grandiose plans, he was stricken by dropsy. This was followed by a stroke. Unable to go on, he was carried toward the Cilician coast. From here, he hoped to sail for Rome.

In the City-on-the-Tiber, the Senate was preparing a welcome that would rival the welcome given to the great Augustus. But, alas, Trajan died at Selinus while on the way in A.D. 117. He was sixty-four. He was cremated and his ashes sent to Rome where they were buried beneath the famous column he had created.

At the time of his death, Trajan had no idea that he would be remembered best because of a letter he had directed against the hated Christians. In his eyes, followers of Christ were too insignificant to even notice!

CHAPTER 12

Bar-Kokhba —the Accepted Messiah

Until recently, the name Bar-Kokhba was either not in the typical Bible dictionary, or it appeared merely as a footnote. With what we know today, this is amazing, for as the leader of the Second Revolt Bar-Kokhba is one of the most colorful personalities in the Christian era. Indeed, he was so colorful many leading rabbis accepted him as the Messiah! Why then, have we known so little about him?

The main answer to that question is that there was no Josephus to record the events of the Second Revolt, as he recorded the events of the First Revolt—the one crushed by Titus.

But today, thanks to archaeology, all of this is changed. One evening in 1960, Prime Minister David Ben-Gurion, Cabinet ministers, and members of the Knesset, with others, met in the home of President Ben Zvi in Jerusalem. Suddenly, as he was flashing pictures on a screen, noted archaeologist Yigael Yadin turned to the President of Israel and said: "Your Excellency, I am honored to be able to tell you that we have discovered fifteen despatches written or dictated by the last President of Israel 1800 years ago" (*Bar-Kokhba* by Yigael Yadin, Random House, 1971).

Bar-Kokhba

Bronze coin shown on page 111 was issued during the Second Revolt. Bar Kokhba made his coinage by stamping his engraving on another coin, usually Roman. This coin is stamped: JERUSALEM.

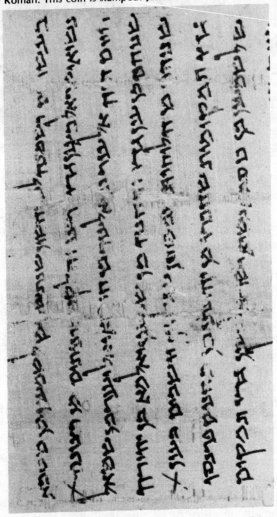

A land-lease in Hebrew from the Bar-Kokhba Revolt (134 C.E.) and discovered at Cave of Letters reads: "On the twenty-eighth day of Marheshvan the third year of Shimeon bar Kosiba, President of Israel; at En-gedi . . ."

This shattering announcement was followed by absolute silence. And then cries of astonishment and joy shook the room. On the following day banner headlines appeared throughout the world.

Since the Jews had been so thoroughly defeated by the Romans in A.D. 70, and since their Temple, the very center of their life and devotion, had been utterly destroyed, it seemed they and their religion were finished forever. But encouraged by their rabbis, and prodded by their gloating conquerors whose bad taste inspired them to issue a coin with *Judaea Capta* inscribed on it, Judaism kept squirming for a new birth.

In A.D. 115 a revolt erupted in Cyrenaica. This was followed by rebellion in Mesopotamia a year later. Thoroughly alarmed, the Romans strangled the uprising through the leadership of a Romanized Moor by the name of L. Quietus. Again, Jewish resistance was brought under control, but it was not eliminated.

Friction between the Jews and Romans continued to increase. And this friction burst into flames when Hadrian extended Domitian's law against castration to include circumcision. This law stirred the Jews to their very depths.

Then in A.D. 132 Simeon Bar-Kokhba made his appearance.

For centuries, Bar-Kokhba had been a semi-real Robin Hood type of hero to Jews all over the world. This is true even though references to him in ancient literature have been few and inconclusive. For centuries in Eastern Europe the Jewish holiday Lag B Omer, commemorating the scholars, has been accompanied by special games staged in the fields by the children. In these games, the children arm themselves and pretend they are either Bar-Kokhba or his Roman enemies.

But today, thanks to the archaeologists, we know that Bar-Kokhba was a real man. And we also know, as Yigael Yadin showed with his slides, that he was the president of an independent Israel.

Bar-Kokhba

By A.D. 132, Bar-Kokhba had gathered an army sufficiently strong to lash out against the Romans. His main problem had been that of arming his men. This he solved by a clever but dishonest ruse. He arranged for his leaders to acquire the rights to supply weapons to the Roman commanders. By design, many of these weapons were of inferior quality. When they were rejected, they were hidden in strategic caves to be ready for the rebellion.

Possessing a magnetic personality, Bar-Kokhba was accepted as the Messiah by many. And among those who felt this way about him was the brilliant Akiba. Concerning this man, a modern Jewish writer has said: "Akiba, who followed Gamaliel, is one of the most famous Jews of all times. Starting late in life, he became the most learned of his fellow rabbis. He was especially expert at basing new rules and decisions on words and passages in the Bible. He was known for his defence of the weaker members of society...." (*The Eternal People* by Charry and Segal, United Synagogue of America, 1967).

Akiba was thoroughly impressed with Bar-Kokhba; and since that name means *Son of a Star,* Akiba connected him with the prophecy of Numbers 24:17—"There shall come a Star out of Jacob, and a Scepter shall rise out of Israel, and shall smite the corners of Moab. . . . " He even went on to say of Bar-Kokhba: *"This is the King Messiah!"*

Bar-Kokhba was an excellent military strategist and disciplinarian. He demanded absolute obedience. Jewish sources claim that he even hacked off the fingers of his followers. When the wise ones asked, "How long will you continue to make the men of Israel blemished?" he answered, "How else shall they be tested?" Impressed, the sages answered, "Let anyone who cannot uproot a cedar from Lebanon be refused enrollment in your army."

These extreme statements may not be completely true,

but there is no doubt that his army—estimated to have numbered 400,000—was an extremely tough army. Bar-Kokhba and his followers also brimmed with confidence. Some records indicate that they were almost blasphemous. "When they went forth to battle, they cried: (O God) neither help us nor disgrace us." This arrogance is surprising, for the items found in the caves which they had hidden indicate that they were devout followers of the Law.

In the beginning of the revolt, Hadrian seemed confident that it would be crushed with minimum effort. The Emperor was mistaken. Bar-Kokhba wiped out an entire Roman legion. And more humiliating still, this legion was the proud Twenty-second Deioterana—determined veterans from Egypt.

Victory after victory followed this Roman defeat. Soon Jerusalem was once again in the hands of the Jews. Animal sacrifices were restored and Bar-Kokhba was proclaimed the leader. Soon he began to issue his own coins, and the inscriptions on coins that have been found indicate his progress.

Stamped on one coin are the words: *Year One of the Redemption of Israel.* On another: *Year Two of the Freedom of Israel.* And yet another has the facade of the Temple with a star above it and the word *Jerusalem* by the side.

Some of the discovered orders of Bar-Kokhba indicate that he was either arrogant because of victory or desperate because of defeat. One order reads: *I take heaven to witness against me that unless you destroy the Galileans who are with you every man, I will put fetters on your feet as I did to ben Aphul.*

During these days of triumph, Eleazar became the High Priest, and Akiba was named the leader of the Sanhedrin.

The Christians had nothing to do with Bar-Kokhba. And perhaps the reason was that they remembered the words of Jesus: "If any man shall say unto you, Lo, here

Bar-Kokhba

is Christ, or there; believe it not. For there shall arise false Christs ... and shall show great signs and wonders; insomuch that, if it were possible, they shall deceive the very elect. . . . Wherefore if they shall say unto you, Behold he is in the desert; go not forth" (Matthew 24:23-26).

And since the Christians would not help him, Bar-Kokhba persecuted them. Eusebius wrote: "In the recent Jewish War, Bar-Kokhba, leader of the Jewish insurrection, ordered the Christians alone to be sentenced to terrible punishments if they did not deny Jesus Christ and blaspheme him."

When Hadrian realized that he was dealing with a military genius, he summoned Julius Severus from his post as governor of Britain and ordered him to end the revolt. Severus realized that he did not know the land with the thoroughness of the Jews and so therefore he avoided pitched battles. Instead, he resorted to siege and the cutting of food supplies.

But even with the might of Rome it took three years to crush the rebellion. The price was appalling. Normally after a victory, the Emperor began his report to the Senate with the words: "If you and your children are in health, it is well; and the legions are in health." But on this occasion, Hadrian omitted the words, *mihi et legionibus bene.*

The Romans, however, did not neglect vengeance. Nearly one thousand Jewish settlements and cities were destroyed, and 580,000 Jews lost their lives. Bar-Kokhba himself was killed by a Samaritan who then cut off his head and sent it to Hadrian.

Fragments of ancient scrolls—some of them doubtful—attribute all kinds of atrocities to the Romans. One of these states that they rolled Jewish children in holy books and then burned them. In addition, the city of Jerusalem was utterly destroyed. But more of that in the next chapter.

What happened to Bar-Kokhba? Even before he was

killed, the people began to lose confidence in him. Some even whispered that his real name was *Bar-Coziba* (Son of Falsehood)!

CHAPTER 13

Hadrian —He Renamed Jerusalem

From the time Jerusalem became a Jewish city thousands of years ago, Jews have revered it with a love that is almost unbelievable. The city has meant more to them than life. Indeed, it has meant so much European Jew-baiters from the Middle Ages on through the days of Hitler have taunted them by shouting *Hep! Hep!*

That seemingly harmless syllable is made from the first letters of the Latin sentence *Hierisilyma est perdita* which means Jerusalem is lost. Such an idea to a Jew is unthinkable. And perhaps because of this confidence, tyrants have again and again sought to hurt the Jews by destroying Jerusalem.

As we have seen, Roman Emperor Titus burned the Temple and razed most of the city in A.D. 70. This is an event the Jews are determined never to forget. And even in our time, in order to remind themselves of that event, a Jewish bridegroom crushes a wineglass beneath his heel in the midst of his wedding ceremony.

Following the destruction of the city in A.D. 70, the Xth Legion was left to control the ruins. The catastrophe of A.D. 135, however, was much more severe. Having defeated Bar-Kokhba, Roman Emperor Hadrian decided to destroy the city forever. His order was that the city

Hadrian

should be plowed over and rebuilt—on Roman lines. And this was just the beginning of the insults that were heaped on the Jews.

The despised figure of a pig was carved over one of the gates in honor of the Xth Legion which had wrecked the city under Titus, a temple to Jupiter Capitolinus was erected at the site of Solomon's Temple, and the statue of Hadrian was stood at the spot once occupied by the Holy of Holies.

The new city received the name Aelia Capitolina. The Aelia glorified the name of the Emperor—Publius Aelius Hadrianus; and the Capitolina was in honor of Capitoline Jupiter—the new patron god of Rome.

All Jews were forbidden to enter the city, and any Jew who did so was immediately crucified. An exception to this rule was made on the ninth day of Ab each year. This was the day the Temple was destroyed. By paying a fee, a Jew was allowed to enter in order to pray for the restoration of the Temple.

Both circumcision and the study of the Law were forbidden. However, Jews converted to Christianity were welcome in the city. But each male who sought admittance could be challenged to show that he had not been circumcised.

Tens of thousands of slaves were taken and shipped to Rome; and since such a vast number flooded the market, the price of a slave fell so low it was cheaper to buy a slave than a horse. As a matter of record, there was such a large supply of slaves many were freed. It was too expensive to feed them while awaiting a buyer.

In renaming and rebuilding Jerusalem, Hadrian sought to stamp out Judaism forever. But as often happens, the evil he intended accomplished a certain amount of good. Indeed, three historic blessings can be attributed to his misdeeds.

1. To divide Jerusalem into sections, two long colonnaded streets were laid out in such a way they crossed in the very center of the city. Thus, they formed

the sign of the cross. This fact caused comment for many a century. Some saw in this the eternal truth that the cross can never be destroyed; others that it supersedes the Mosaic Law.

2. One of Hadrian's motives was to stamp out all sacred places in Jerusalem. To do this, he sought to obliterate them by erecting pagan shrines on the same sites. But in doing so, he merely marked the spots for future generations. Thus, his pagan shrines identified the ancient location of the Temple and other such renowned places.

3. Until Hadrian's time, Christianity was considered by the uninformed to be merely a sect of Judaism. Then, due to Hadrian's edict about Jews entering the city, the division between the two was clearly indicated. For by affirming that they were not followers of Judaism, Christians were allowed access to the city.

As a final blow to the Jews, Hadrian renamed the province of Judea. His new name was Palestina, in honor of the Philistines! (Actually, Hadrian merely legalized this name for it had been used before, by Herodotus in the fifth century B.C.).

Today, not much can be seen of the ruins of Aelia Capitolina. But archaeologists have been able to trace its approximate setting, and occasionally a piece of tile or fragment of a drain shows up. The main north gate of the Roman city was the Damascus Gate. This is known because of an inscription of Herod Agrippa just above the gateway.

The inside story of how Hadrian became emperor may never be known. Roman gossip had it that since Trajan died without a natural heir, his widow Plotina managed to get Hadrian onto the throne because she was in love with him. Both Hadrian and Plotina denied this, but the story remained in circulation during his entire reign. Forty-one-year-old Hadrian was, however, Trajan's second cousin and nearest relative. At the time of his election, he was governor of Syria and was living in

Hadrian

Hadrian's tomb is a prominent building in Rome.

Antioch.

Hadrian was tall, elegant, and physically strong. Also, he made beards popular by growing one himself. He loved the arts, wrote several books including an autobiography, painted, and was a fair sculptor. But his main passion was to build walls and new cities. And because of this building mania he even built tombs for his beloved dogs.

Hadrian was born in Italy. But then his family moved to Spain. Perhaps it was this that interested him in travel. And because he was a talented administrator, he was able to be away from Rome for as much as five years at a time. As he traveled, he always traveled with experts. In England, he marked one of his frontiers by a wall. Some of the ruins of this wall still remain. This mighty Hadrian Wall was seventy-three miles long, ten feet thick at the base, and twenty feet high. It was also completely fortified.

While in Athens, he was appalled at the lack of employment, and so he began to construct magnificent new buildings. These buildings, designed in the finest Greek fashion, included libraries, temples, and gymnasiums. He also threaded the country with aqueducts. By the time he left, Athens was probably the most beautiful city in the Empire.

Hadrian was superstitious and promoted the old Roman faiths. Actually, however, he had little personal concern with religion. But he is remembered for a letter which in essence was a breakthrough for Christians. Wrote Hadrian:

"To Minucius Fundanus. I have received a letter written to me by His Excellency Serennius Granianus, your predecessor. It is not my intention to leave the matter uninvestigated, for fear of causing the men embarrassment and abetting the informers in their mischiefmaking. If then the provincials can so clearly establish their case against the Christians that they can sustain it in a court of law, let them resort to this

Hadrian

procedure only, and not rely on petitions and mere clamor. Much the most satisfactory course, if anyone should wish to prosecute, is for you to decide the matter. So if someone prosecutes them and proves them guilty of any illegality, you must pronounce sentence according to the seriousness of the offence. *But if anyone starts such proceedings in the hope of financial reward, then for goodness sake arrest him for his shabby trick, and see that he gets his deserts.* " (Italics added. *History of the Church* by Eusebius.)

One wonders what would have happened to Judas Iscariot if this law had been in effect at the time he identified Jesus for thirty pieces of silver!

Hadrian, in spite of his slaughter of the Jews, was concerned with law and mercy. Thus, historians include him as one of the "five good emperors." Once when he told a woman that he didn't have time to listen to her case, she replied: "Don't be an emperor, then." And instead of having her executed, as would have many another emperor, he listened to her problems.

Soon after the Jewish war, Hadrian was stricken with a disease that resembled a combination of tuberculosis and dropsy. Treatment did not help. Again and again he suffered prolonged nosebleeds. He had already prepared his well-known tomb and he longed to occupy it. But death eluded him.

Hadrian requested his doctor to poison him. Instead, the doctor committed suicide. Next, he asked a slave to stab him, but the slave ran away. He then decided to kill himself and demanded either poison or a sword. His frightened servants refused to comply. He then located a dagger on his own and was about to stab himself when it was snatched away.

Desperate to die, Hadrian moved to Baiae and deliberately ate foods he believed to be injurious to his health. Eventually, his longed-for death came on July 10, 138. His body was cremated and his ashes were deposited in his tomb.

After Hadrian's death, a number of senators who had been awaiting execution were released. His successor Antoninus pled with the Senate to confer divine honors on him. At first this request was refused, but when the elected emperor refused to take the throne until the honors were voted, the Senate reluctantly agreed. Thus, it was voted that Hadrian was a god.

Like Hadrian, Antoninus was famous for building a wall in Britain. His wall, together with the one erected by Hadrian, made Britain safe for Rome for the next two centuries. But the decay which would eventually topple the Empire had already started its deadly work. The good news of Jesus Christ, however, has continued to spread. Moreover, its power and virility have remained.

The story of these tyrants of New Testament times is a bloody tale of incest, perversion, adultery, murder, greed, war, countless executions—and abject misery. In stark contrast, the story of the Christians whom they persecuted is a story of joy, success, transformation. All of this reminds one of a favorite hymn written by Sabine Baring-Gould. The third verse goes like this:

Crowns and thrones may perish, Kingdoms rise and wane,
But the church of Jesus Constant will remain;
Gates of hell can never 'Gainst that church prevail
We have Christ's own promise, And that cannot fail.

Selected Bibliography

A vast amount of information is available on the subjects in this book. Research included study in many libraries and the use of inter-library loans. The following books have been especially useful and are recommended for the general reader.

Blaiklock, E. M., *The Zondervan Pictorial Bible Atlas,* 1969.

Durant, Will, *Caesar and Christ,* Simon and Schuster, 1944.

Encyclopedia Judaica, Macmillan Company, 1972.

Eusebius, *The History of the Church from Christ to Constantine,* translated by G. A. Williamson, Penguin Classics, 1965.

Interpreter's Dictionary of the Bible, Abingdon, 1962.

Josephus, Flavius, *The Life and Works of Flavius Josephus,* Winston.

Perowne, Stewart, *Life and Times of Herod the Great,* Abingdon, 1959.

Pliny the Younger, *Letters,* Loeb Library.

Sandmel, Samuel, *Herod, Profile of a Tyrant,* Lippincott, 1967.

Suetonius, *The Twelve Caesars,* translated by Robert Graves and published by Penguin Books, 1957.

Tenney, Merrill C. *Pictorial Bible Dictionary,* Zondervan, 1963.

The New Schaff-Herzog Encyclopedia of Religious

Knowledge, Baker Book House, 1960.

Yadin, Yigael, *Bar-Kokhba,* Random House, 1971.